- Go to **awmi.net/sg440** to download PDFs of the following resources for each lesson in this study guide:
    - Outlines
    - Discipleship Questions
    - Scriptures
- Share as many copies as you'd like.
- These documents are not for resale.

DON'T LIMIT GOD

Imagine Yourself Successful

STUDY GUIDE

Andrew Wommack

Unless otherwise indicated, all Scripture quotations are taken from the *King James Version* of the Bible.

The author has emphasized some words in Scripture throughout this study guide.

Don't Limit God Study Guide
ISBN: 978-1-59548-229-7
Item Code: 440

awmi.net

TABLE OF CONTENTS

HOW TO USE YOUR STUDY GUIDE

Whether you are teaching a class, leading a small group, discipling an individual, or studying on your own, this study guide is designed for you! Here's how it works:

Each Lesson consists of the **Lesson** text, **Outline**, **Teacher's Guide**, **Discipleship Questions**, **Answer Key**, and **Scriptures**—some of which have been divided into sections. Some studies also have additional information.

Outline for Group Study:

I.   If possible, briefly review the previous study by going over the **Answer Key/Teacher's Guide** answers for the **Discipleship Questions/Teacher's Guide** questions.

II. Read the current **Lesson** text or **Teacher's Guide** aloud (or section—e.g., 1.1, 1.2, etc.).
   A.   Be sure that each student has a copy of the **Outline**.
   B.   While the **Lesson** text, **Teacher's Guide**, or section is being read, students should use their **Outlines** to follow along.

III. Once the **Lesson** text, **Teacher's Guide**, or section is read, facilitate discussion and study using the **Discipleship Questions/Teacher's Guide** questions (all questions are the same).
   A.   Read aloud one question at a time.
   B.   The group should use their **Outlines** to assist them in answering the questions.
   C.   Have them read aloud each specifically mentioned scripture before answering the question.
   D.   Discuss the answer/point from the **Lesson** text, as desired.
   E.   As much as possible, keep the discussion centered on the scriptures and the **Lesson** text, **Teacher's Guide**, or section points at hand.
   F.   Remember, the goal is understanding (Matt. 13:19).
   G.   One individual should not dominate the discussion; instead, try to draw out the quieter ones for the group conversation.
   H.   Repeat the process until all of the questions are discussed/answered.

Materials Needed:

Study guide, Bible, and enough copies of the **Outline, Discipleship Questions,** and **Scriptures** for each student. (PDFs of the **Outlines, Discipleship Questions,** and **Scriptures** can be downloaded via the URL located on the first page of this study guide.)

Outline for Personal Study:

I. Read the current **Lesson** text, **Teacher's Guide**, or section.
   A. Read additional information, if provided.
   B. Meditate on the given scriptures, as desired.
II. Answer the corresponding **Discipleship Questions/Teacher's Guide** questions.
III. Check your work with the **Answer Key/Teacher's Guide** answers.

Materials Needed:

Study guide, Bible, and a writing utensil.

INTRODUCTION

March 23, 1968. Many of you have heard me talk about this date as being the most significant one of my life and ministry. On that day, I had an encounter with the Lord that completely changed the way I viewed God. As a result, I became a new person and the vision for my ministry was birthed.

But there is another date you may not have heard about: January 31, 2002. On that day, God spoke to me from Psalm 78 and told me that my small thinking had been limiting what He wanted to do in my life. I had no idea I was limiting Him, but I made an immediate decision to change my thinking. I made the decision to take the limits off God.

At the time the Lord spoke to me, the ministry was only reaching 6 percent of the American television market. Now the *Gospel Truth* television program completely covers the U.S. market and most of the English-speaking world, and reaches over 3 billion people. We have grown exponentially in many other areas as well—all because I dared to take the limits off God and believe Him for the bigger things He had wanted to do all along. We would definitely not be where we are today had I continued to limit the Lord with my small thinking.

WRONG BELIEFS

D o you know that chances are, you are limiting God? Most people limit God in one way or another. There are many things that can hinder—or limit—what God can do in your life. One area in which people limit God is through their wrong beliefs. Many think that God is in total control and that everything that happens is His will. They blame Him for everything while having a fatalistic theology that says everything that happens must somehow or other be God's plan or purpose for their lives. If their marriages fail, they think maybe it's God's way of breaking them or humbling them. If their businesses fail, they accept this as God's will.

When I went to India in 1980, it was a total culture shock, but I learned a lot. One thing I learned was that India is really a very rich country. In fact, it's one of the most populous places on the face of the earth and has an abundance of natural resources. India's lack of prosperity isn't due to finances or resources; it's because of their belief system.

When I was in India, I noticed that people were literally starving to death while "meat" roamed through their homes. I was actually in a house, holding a Bible study, when a Brahman bull walked in the door. Everyone pressed against the wall and let this big Brahman bull do whatever he wanted—all because Hindus believe the animal could be someone's reincarnated grandmother. The Hindu people won't eat beef, but they will eat some "lower" forms of meat, such as dogs or goats, because they believe these animals represent the reincarnation of lower life forms.

The Hindu people have resources that could end their hunger, but their religious belief system limits them. They also believe that they are born into a caste system, and if they do anything to try to get out of it and improve their well-being, they might be reincarnated as an ant or something worse. Their belief system has impoverished their nation and limited them.

Many Americans attempt to go into different cultures and simply throw money at the problems, thinking that will solve everything. Yet money is not the problem in India or anywhere else; it's the belief system of the culture. People need the Gospel, as well as a set of principles and a moral code, which will cause them to change their belief system. Once these things are put in place, nations will begin to prosper. A culture's belief system will limit its people and keep them in poverty.

Likewise, many people in America think the government owes them welfare, needs to increase their pay or benefits, and should give them more guaranteed health insurance. That is not our problem. Our problem is right between our ears—the way we think and believe. Proverbs 23:7 tells us that as a man thinks in his heart, so is he.

Our lives go the way of our thoughts (Rom. 12:2). If we want to change, we shouldn't pray that somebody will just give us more money, nor should we take money from somebody who has it and give it to those who don't. That's not our answer. Our answer is to start taking the limits off our wrong thinking because the way we think in our hearts will direct the course of our lives. We need to change ourselves—our thinking, our mindsets—if we want to take the limits off God.

YOU HAVE A SPHERE OF INFLUENCE

God is no respecter of persons (Acts 10:34). He wants to do absolutely miraculous things in everyone's life. God has never made a piece of junk. He has never made an inferior person. We all have something that God wants to accomplish through us, but most of us are ignorant of this and have bought into the lie that there's nothing special about us. But the truth is that we are all unique and can do something that nobody else can.

> *For I know the thoughts that I think toward you, saith the* LORD, *thoughts of peace, and not of evil, to give you an expected end.*
> JEREMIAH 29:11

God has good thoughts toward each of us. He has a perfect plan for our lives. We are *"fearfully and wonderfully made"* (Ps. 139:14). Whether our parents saw us coming or not, God knew us from the foundation of the world and has a purpose for us. Yet most of us are living way below God's standard and limiting what He wants to do in our lives.

I spend over a million dollars on television airtime each month. Our ministry is increasing and we are going to keep spending more, but even if we spend $10 million a month, there are many people who will never hear of me or my ministry, no matter how much money I pour into television. You have the ability to impact people whom I will never reach.

We all have a sphere of influence, or people whom we can reach. These are people who know us and are watching us—family members, neighbors, friends, and coworkers—who will die and go to hell if we just sit around and wait for our pastors or another minister to talk to them. We need to rise up and let God use us to touch these people and help us reach our full potential!

Whenever I ask how many people are called to be leaders, there are always those who don't raise their hands. They do not see themselves as leaders. But they are. Leadership is defined as influence, and all of them have influence over someone—whether it's their kids, neighbors, or friends. Some of them have more influence than others, but all of them are called to influence someone. If they don't see themselves as leaders having influence over others and rather think, *Oh, poor me, whatever will be will be,* then they are going through life like a pinball. They are just bouncing from problem to problem and whatever else they happen to bump into without any course for their lives. They need to take their God-given authority and command mountains to move. If they don't, they are limiting God.

God made everyone to be a leader. This can vary according to your specific call. But if you have God Almighty living inside of you, He has a purpose for your life that will cause you to accomplish things and influence people in a way that will satisfy you. Many of you aren't influencing people in a positive way, and your life is not accomplishing anything. If you are born again, then God is living on the inside of you, and He has something important for you to do. God doesn't just sovereignly make everything work. If your life is not an absolute joy and you aren't excited about it—if you don't have enthusiasm about your life or where you're going or what God is doing—you have missed God and are limiting what He wants to do in your life.

GOD CALLED YOU TO DO SOMETHING BEYOND YOURSELF

When God spoke to me on January 31, 2002, out of Psalm 78, it revolutionized my life. This psalm was written for the younger generation to see what the older generation did—so they could learn not to limit God and not to grieve Him like their parents did. This is powerful! The Lord used this psalm to completely change my life.

> *Yea, they turned back and tempted God, and limited the Holy One of Israel.*
>
> PSALM 78:41

God spoke this very simple passage to me in 2002, and I pray that He speaks this to you too. No one has exhausted God's ability, resources, or power for their lives. God is infinite. God is huge. Your life ought to be a reflection of that. If you can look at your life and say "Well, I went to school, I did this and that, and I earned the things I have," you have missed God. Your life should be such a testimony that when people ask how you're doing, what you're doing, and why you're so blessed, you can only say that there's no explanation outside of God. If you can point to your great education, your charisma, or your ability, then you have missed God. If your life isn't supernatural, it's superficial.

God will call you to do something that is beyond yourself. He will call you to do something that is bigger than yourself. If it's something you can do on your own, I doubt you have heard from God. For instance, God called me to preach the Word while I was an introvert. I couldn't look someone in the face and talk to them when I was in high school, but now I speak to millions and millions of people. God called me to do something that is absolutely beyond me!

God had me do things that there's no human explanation for. I don't have an answer to why God's blessings are so big on my ministry. It's beyond my natural ability. I'm not doing anything except loving Jesus and holding on to Him. I can't point to my ministry and tell you that it's blessed because of my great talent or ability. As a matter of fact, if I were God, I wouldn't have chosen me.

YOU AREN'T SMART ENOUGH TO DO IT ON YOUR OWN!

For ye see your calling, brethren, how that not many wise men after the flesh, not many mighty, not many noble, are called.

1 CORINTHIANS 1:26

That's me—I qualify. You cannot point to my ministry and say its success is because of my great talents or abilities. I am not doing anything that I can do on my own. Everything that's being accomplished is because of God working through me.

My mother died in 2009 when she was ninety-six years old. Right before she died, she asked me how the ministry was doing. I told her about all of the awesome things God was doing in America and overseas. She looked at me and, pointing her bony little finger at me, said, "Andy, you know that's God."

I said, "Yes, ma'am, I know it's God."

She said, "You aren't smart enough to do that."

I said, "Guilty! Amen. It's true."

If you can say that you've achieved everything by your own ability, strength, or power, then you have not yet tapped into God's will for your life. God will ask you to do something bigger than yourself—something that requires more than your own ability.

All of us have missed God at some point in our lives. We are not hitting on every single cylinder. None of us are believing God as we should or doing everything we are supposed to be doing. God is big, limitless, and infinite. He wants us to believe for big things, yet most of us only believe for small things.

When God spoke to me in 2002, He told me that I was limiting Him just like the Israelites who turned back in their hearts and limited the Holy One of Israel (Ps. 78:41). I honestly had no idea I was limiting God. Prior to Him speaking to me, I had been in ministry for thirty-four years and had seen many incredible things happen. I'd seen miracles, including people being raised from the dead. I had even seen my own son raised from the dead. He had been dead for five hours, yet he had no brain damage—well, at least no more than before!

If you believe that God is sovereign and can do whatever He wants, then you might just have to tear Psalm 78 from your Bible. That psalm says that the Israelites limited God. God wanted to do more than they would let Him do. God wanted to bring them into the Promised Land—and He wanted to do it in one year, not forty! But the Israelites sent spies out who said there were giants in the land. They refused to go and, therefore, delayed God's will for that nation for forty years. They limited God!

We don't have to go beyond the children of Israel to see that we can limit God. God did not want the Israelites to spend forty years in the wilderness, yet they limited Him because of their fear of man. We can apply this same principle to other areas of our lives, such as healing. According to 3 John 2, God does not want us sick, yet we often limit God in how He can heal us.

> *And Moses was an hundred and twenty years old when he died: his eye was not dim, nor his natural force abated.*
>
> DEUTERONOMY 34:7

Moses was strong and had perfect eyesight when he was 120 years old. If God will do that for a person in the Old Covenant, just imagine how much more He will do for us who are under the New Covenant. We limit God when we think, *I'm over 40, so this is just normal. Things are supposed to start going wrong in my body, and my eyesight is supposed to start going dim.* We compare ourselves with others (2 Cor. 10:12) and say, "This is the way it's supposed to be." But we need to look at the Word of God and believe that we can be strong like Moses and have good eyesight. We limit God by thinking that things have to be a certain way simply because that's what others are experiencing.

If thou shalt say in thine heart, These nations are more than I; how can I dispossess them?

This verse is exactly what I was saying when God told me I was limiting Him. The Israelites limited God by saying that the other nations were mightier than they were. God promised them absolute victory, but they wavered and began to doubt His promise. When they did that, they limited God and He couldn't drive the nations out (Heb. 4:2).

LESSON 1.1 • WRONG BELIEFS
OUTLINE

I.   Chances are, you are limiting God.
  A. One area in which you limit Him is through your wrong beliefs.
  B. Many think that God is in total control and that everything that happens is His will.
      i.   If their marriages fail, they think that He is breaking them or humbling them.
      ii. If their businesses fail, they accept this as His will.
  C. People need the Gospel, as well as a set of principles and a moral code, which will cause them to change their belief system.
      i.   Once these things are put in place, they will begin to prosper.
  D. The way you think in your heart will direct the course of your life (Prov. 23:7 and Rom. 12:2).

II. We all have something that God wants to accomplish through us.
  A. Most of us have bought into the lie that there's nothing special about us.
      i.   God has good thoughts toward each of us (Jer. 29:11).
      ii. We are fearfully and wonderfully made (Ps. 139:14).
  B. Most of us are living way below God's standard and limiting what He wants to do in our lives.
  C. There are people we know who will die and go to hell if we just sit around and wait for our pastors or another minister to talk to them.
  D. We need to rise up and let God use us to touch people and help us reach our full potential!

III. All of us are leaders.
  A. Leadership is defined as influence, and all of us have influence over someone.
  B. Some of us have more influence than others, but all of us are called to influence someone.
  C. God doesn't just sovereignly make everything work.

IV. God used Psalm 78:41 to revolutionize my life:

     Yea, they turned back and tempted God, and limited the Holy One of Israel.

  A. No one has exhausted God's ability, resources, or power for their lives—He is huge.
  B. If you can point to your great education, your charisma, or your ability when people ask how you're doing what you're doing and why you're so blessed, then you have missed God.
  C. If your life isn't supernatural, it's superficial.
  D. God will call you to do something bigger than yourself.

E. God called me to preach the Word while I was an introvert—I couldn't look someone in the face and talk to them when I was in high school, but now I speak to millions and millions of people.

F. God had me do things that there's no human explanation for.

G. I don't have an answer to why God's blessings are so big on my ministry.

H. I'm not doing anything except loving Jesus and holding on to Him.

V. All of us have missed God at some point in our lives.

A. None of us are believing God as we should or doing everything we are supposed to be doing.

B. He wants us to believe for big things, yet most of us only believe for small things.

C. If we believe that God is sovereign and can do whatever He wants, then we might just have to tear Psalm 78 from our Bibles (see Ps. 78:41).

D. When the Israelites refused to go into the Promised Land, they limited God because of their fear of man.

VI. We can apply this principle—fear limits God—to other areas of our lives, such as healing.

A. According to 3 John 2, God does not want us sick, yet we often limit God in how He can heal us.

B. Moses was strong and had perfect eyesight when he was 120 years old (Deut. 34:7).

C. If God will do that for a person in the Old Covenant, just imagine how much more He will do for us who are under the New Covenant.

D. We limit God by thinking that things have to be a certain way because that's what others are experiencing.

> *If thou shalt say in thine heart, These nations are more than I; how can I dispossess them?*
> DEUTERONOMY 7:17

E. This verse is exactly what I was saying when God told me I was limiting Him.

F. God promised the Israelites absolute victory, but they wavered and began to doubt His promise.

G. When they did that, they limited God and He couldn't drive the nations out (Heb. 4:2).

LESSON 1.1 • WRONG BELIEFS
TEACHER'S GUIDE

1.   Chances are, we are limiting God. One area in which we limit Him is through our wrong beliefs. Many of us think that God is in total control and that everything that happens is His will. If our marriages fail, we think that He is breaking us or humbling us. If our businesses fail, we accept this as His will. We need the Gospel, as well as a set of principles and a moral code, which will cause us to change our belief system. Once these things are put in place, we will begin to prosper. The way we think in our hearts will direct the course of our lives (Prov. 23:7 and Rom. 12:2).

1a.   One area in which you limit God is through your what?
   Wrong beliefs

1b.   True or false: God is in total control, and everything that happens is His will.
   False

1c.   What are some things that need to be put into place for you to begin to change your beliefs and begin to prosper?
   The Gospel, a set of principles, and a moral code

1d.   The course of your life is directed by what?
   A.   The career path you chose
   B.   The plan that God has chosen for you
   C.   The way you think in your heart
   D.   All of the above
   E.   None of the above
   C.   The way you think in your heart

2. We all have something that God wants to accomplish through us. Most of us have bought into the lie that there's nothing special about us. God has good thoughts toward each of us (Jer. 29:11). We are fearfully and wonderfully made (Ps. 139:14). Most of us are living way below God's standard and limiting what He wants to do in our lives. There are people we know who will die and go to hell if we just sit around and wait for our pastors or another minister to talk to them. We need to rise up and let God use us to touch people and help us reach our full potential!

2a. Everyone has something that God wants to _____ through them.
   Accomplish
2b. Compared to God's standard, where do most people live?
   A. Just at
   B. Way below
   C. Way above
   D. Comparable to others
   E. On the right path
   B. Way below
2c. *Discussion question:* How does letting God use you not only help others but also help you reach your full potential?
   Discussion question

3. All of us are leaders. Leadership is defined as influence, and all of us have influence over someone. Some of us have more influence than others, but all of us are called to influence someone. God doesn't just sovereignly make everything work.

3a. True or false: If leadership is defined as influence, all of us are leaders.
   True
3b. Everyone is called to _____.
   A. Be prophets
   B. The pastorate
   C. Politics
   D. The mission field
   E. Influence people
   E. Influence people
3c. *Discussion question:* What does it mean that God doesn't sovereignly work everything out?
   Discussion question

4.   God used Psalm 78:41 to revolutionize Andrew's life:

> *Yea, they turned back and tempted God, and limited the Holy One of Israel.*

We have not exhausted God's ability, resources, or power for our lives—He is huge. If we can point to our great educations, our charisma, or our abilities when people ask how we're doing what we're doing and why we're so blessed, then we have missed God. If our lives aren't supernatural, they're superficial. God will call us to do something bigger than ourselves. God called Andrew to preach the Word while he was an introvert—he couldn't look someone in the face and talk to them when he was in high school, but now he speaks to millions and millions of people. God had Andrew do things that there's no human explanation for. He doesn't have an answer to why God's blessings are so big on his ministry. He's not doing anything except loving Jesus and holding on to Him.

4a. Because God is huge, what can you not exhaust?
  A. God's ability
  B. God's resources
  C. God's power
  D. All of the above
  E. None of the above
  D. All of the above
4b. If someone asks you why you are so blessed and you point to your education, charisma, or ability, why have you missed it?
  God will do something bigger than you that requires more than your own ability
4c. *Discussion question:* Why does Andrew say that if your life isn't supernatural, it's superficial?
  Discussion question

5.   All of us have missed God at some point in our lives. None of us are believing God as we should or doing everything we are supposed to be doing. He wants us to believe for big things, yet most of us only believe for small things. If we believe that God is sovereign and can do whatever He wants, then we might just have to tear Psalm 78 from our Bibles (see Ps. 78:41). When the Israelites refused to go into the Promised Land, they limited God because of their fear of man.

5a. True or false: Most people are believing God for big things and are doing everything they should be doing.
  False
5b. *Discussion question:* Read Psalm 78:41. How does believing that God is sovereign limit Him?
  Discussion question
5c. What limited God and stopped the Israelites from going into the Promised Land?
  Their fear of man

6. We can apply this principle—fear limits God—to other areas of our lives, such as healing. According to 3 John 2, God does not want us sick, yet we often limit God in how He can heal us. Moses was strong and had perfect eyesight when he was 120 years old (Deut. 34:7). If God will do that for a person in the Old Covenant, we should just imagine how much more He will do for us who are under the New Covenant. We limit God by thinking that things have to be a certain way because that's what others are experiencing.

> *If thou shalt say in thine heart, These nations are more than I; how can I dispossess them?*
> DEUTERONOMY 7:17

This verse is exactly what Andrew was saying when God told him he was limiting Him. God promised the Israelites absolute victory, but they wavered and began to doubt His promise. When they did that, they limited God and He couldn't drive the nations out (Heb. 4:2).

6a. True or false: According to 3 John 2, God sometimes wants you to be sick if it will help your soul prosper.
False

6b. You limit God by _____ that things have to be a certain way because that's what others are _____.
Thinking / experiencing

6c. True or false: God promised the Israelites absolute victory in their battles.
True

6d. The Israelites limited what God could do for them when they _____.
   A. Wavered and began to doubt
   B. Believed and began to shout
   C. Fasted and began to pray
   D. All of the above
   E. None of the above
   A. Wavered and began to doubt

LESSON 1.1 • WRONG BELIEFS
DISCIPLESHIP QUESTIONS

1. One area in which you limit God is through your what?

   _____

   _____

   _____

2. True or false: God is in total control, and everything that happens is His will.

3. What are some things that need to be put into place for you to begin to change your beliefs and begin to prosper?

   _____

   _____

   _____

4. The course of your life is directed by what?
   A. The career path you choose
   B. The plan that God has chosen for you
   C. The way you think in your heart
   D. All of the above
   E. None of the above

5. Everyone has something that God wants to _____ through them.

6. Compared to God's standard, where do most people live?
   A. Just at
   B. Way below
   C. Way above
   D. Comparable to others
   E. On the right path

7. *Discussion question:* How does letting God use you not only help others but also help you reach your full potential?

   _____

   _____

   _____

DON'T LIMIT GOD

8. True or false: If leadership is defined as influence, all of us are leaders.

9. Everyone is called to _____.
   A. Be prophets
   B. The pastorate
   C. Politics
   D. The mission field
   E. Influence people

10. *Discussion question*: What does it mean that God doesn't sovereignly work everything out?
    _____
    _____
    _____

11. Because God is huge, what can you not exhaust?
    A. God's ability
    B. God's resources
    C. God's power
    D. All of the above
    E. None of the above

12. If someone asks you why you are so blessed and you point to your education, charisma, or ability, why have you missed it?
    _____
    _____
    _____

13. *Discussion question*: Why does Andrew say that if your life isn't supernatural, it's superficial?
    _____
    _____
    _____

14. True or false: Most people are believing God for big things and are doing everything they should be doing.

15. *Discussion question:* Read Psalm 78:41. How does believing that God is sovereign limit Him?

_____

_____

_____

16. What limited God and stopped the Israelites from going into the Promised Land?

_____

_____

_____

17. True or false: According to 3 John 2, God sometimes wants you to be sick if it will help your soul prosper.

18. You limit God by _____ that things have to be a certain way because that's what others are _____.

19. True or false: God promised the Israelites absolute victory in their battles.

20. The Israelites limited what God could do for them when they _____.
    A. Wavered and began to doubt
    B. Believed and began to shout
    C. Fasted and began to pray
    D. All of the above
    E. None of the above

LESSON 1.1 • WRONG BELIEFS

ANSWER KEY

1. Wrong beliefs
2. False
3. The Gospel, a set of principles, and a moral code
4. C. The way you think in your heart
5. Accomplish
6. B. Way below
7. *Discussion question*
8. True
9. E. Influence people
10. *Discussion question*
11. D. All of the above
12. God will do something bigger than you that requires more than your own ability
13. *Discussion question*
14. False
15. *Discussion question*
16. Their fear of man
17. False
18. Thinking / experiencing
19. True
20. A. Wavered and began to doubt

LESSON 1.1 • WRONG BELIEFS

SCRIPTURES

PROVERBS 23:7

For as he thinketh in his heart, so is he: Eat and drink, saith he to thee; but his heart is not with thee.

ROMANS 12:2

And be not conformed to this world: but be ye transformed by the renewing of your mind, that ye may prove what is that good, and acceptable, and perfect, will of God.

ACTS 10:34

Then Peter opened his mouth, and said, Of a truth I perceive that God is no respecter of persons.

JEREMIAH 29:11

For I know the thoughts that I think toward you, saith the Lord, thoughts of peace, and not of evil, to give you an expected end.

PSALM 139:14

I will praise thee; for I am fearfully and wonderfully made: marvellous are thy works; and that my soul knoweth right well.

PSALM 78:41

Yea, they turned back and tempted God, and limited the Holy One of Israel.

1 CORINTHIANS 1:26

For ye see your calling, brethren, how that not many wise men after the flesh, not many mighty, not many noble, are called.

3 JOHN 2

Beloved, I wish above all things that thou mayest prosper and be in health, even as thy soul prospereth.

DEUTERONOMY 34:7

And Moses was an hundred and twenty years old when he died: his eye was not dim, nor his natural force abated.

---

2 CORINTHIANS 10:12

For we dare not make ourselves of the number, or compare ourselves with some that commend themselves: but they measuring themselves by themselves, and comparing themselves among themselves, are not wise.

DEUTERONOMY 7:17

If thou shalt say in thine heart, These nations are more than I; how can I dispossess them?

HEBREWS 4:2

For unto us was the gospel preached, as well as unto them: but the word preached did not profit them, not being mixed with faith in them that heard it.

WRONG BELIEFS

Now unto him that is able to do exceeding abundantly above all that we ask or think, according to the power that worketh in us.

EPHESIANS 3:20

Many people use this verse to say that God is able to do anything, but they miss the point. This verse doesn't just say that God is able to do exceeding abundantly above all they ask or think; it goes on to say, *"According to the power that worketh in us." "According to"* means in proportion to or to the degree of the power that is working within.

If we don't have faith and if we are not building ourselves up on our most holy faith (Jude 20), we limit the power of God that flows from us. We can stop the power of God in our lives. If we're not healed, it's not God who didn't heal us—it's us not releasing the power of God on the inside of us. God has to flow through us. When we say that God just sovereignly moved, we are saying that no person had anything to do with His moving. We are saying that God just sovereignly reached down from heaven and did something. That is not scriptural. God always uses people. God flows through people, but there are many ways that we can limit what God wants to do in our lives.

God doesn't move in waves. If we look hard enough, we will find that somebody was praying, somebody was believing God, or somebody was actively involved in bringing about a move of God. There was the Charismatic Movement, the Healing Movement, and the Word of Faith Movement. Yet we blame God as if He's the one who comes in waves and pours out His power then retreats and lets a generation languish. That's not the way God operates. God wants every single person to walk in His fullness.

God would pour out all of these movements at once if we would receive them that way. For instance, in the healing revival, the church had lost the truth of healing. There were some people, like Oral Roberts, who just pressed in. His testimony shows that it didn't *come upon* him—he pursued it.

DON'T LIMIT GOD

I remember Oral Roberts talking about the very first meeting he held. He was so sick and tired of seeing the powerlessness and the lack of healing in the body of Christ, he determined, "I'm not going to live this way. Either the Word is true and God does miracles today, or I'm gonna quit serving God and quit playing the pastor game." He had to fight through unbelief and struggles, but when he began seeing miracles happen, he caught on fire and set others on fire too.

That and other similar instances produced the Healing Movement. People started saying that God was moving in this Healing Movement. God wants to move in healing all the time, but most people won't pursue it the way those involved in these movements did. They broke through in the area of healing and started seeing God's miraculous healing power. However, they didn't break through in other areas. It wasn't that God only wanted to pour out the Healing Movement; He would have poured out the Word Movement, the Charismatic Movement, the Righteousness Movement, and the Baptism in the Holy Spirit Movement all at one time if people would have received them that way.

If we get sick and tired of being sick and tired and decide to start believing God, we will see things happen. We might be tempted to think God is doing a new thing, but no, God is doing the same thing He's wanted to do for 2,000 years. He didn't want the church to go through the Dark Ages—a time when the body of Christ perished for lack of knowledge, not knowing what the Word of God said. If we'll stop limiting Him, He *can* do what He's always wanted.

LIFE IS NOT A DRESS REHEARSAL

God wants to move and bring you into your Promised Land. God wants to do things in your life that will cause you to wake up every day, saying, "God, this is absolutely awesome. You are awesome! What a privilege to be a part of what You are doing." God wants everyone to live this way, yet most just wake up and say, "Oh, great. It's morning; I wish I could go back to bed. It's Monday, and I have to go to work." Or they'll go in to work and say, "TGIF!"

One day I walked through our break room and heard one of our employees say, "TGIF," so I asked him what that meant.

He said, "Thank God it's Friday!"

I asked him what was so good about Fridays. He said, "It's the last day of the work week, and I'm off tomorrow. I don't have to come to work."

I asked him, "Do you not like working here? I could fix it so you don't have to work here."

He said, "Oh, no, I like working here. I just really enjoy my weekend."

I said, "Well, you know what, there's a hundred people who would like your job. If you don't like working here, I could just fix it so every day could be Friday for you."

Boy, did he ever start backpedaling! Of course, I was just kidding him, but you know, if you're not excited about getting up on Monday and going to work or if you get excited on Friday because you don't have to work the next two days, you haven't found God's will for your life. This is one of the ways you limit God in your life. If you're working some dead-end job because you need a pension or job security, then you are missing God.

Life is not a dress rehearsal; it is the real thing. If you aren't doing something with your life that winds you up and fulfills you—something that makes you think, *What a blessing of God this is in my life*—then you have wasted a day of your life. God has a purpose for you, and when you find it, you will be fulfilled. God didn't call everyone to be on television or to stand in front of people like He did me, but He did make everyone special and call them to do something that would fill their lives with joy and peace. If you aren't there, you are wasting time.

Some of you are praying for your life to be different, and you have no joy. You're depressed because you aren't doing what God called you to do. God is pulling you in one direction, but you are going another way because that's what everyone in your family has done for generations. You're afraid that if you turn your life over to God, He might send you to Africa, so you follow logic instead of God. But you won't find joy and fulfillment, because you're not doing what God called you to do.

YOU'RE THE ONE!

Over the past years, I have ministered to a business with about thirty employees in Charlotte, North Carolina. The owner gathers his staff and tells them, "The clock is running. I'm paying you to listen to this man for as long as he wants to talk." Then I share the Word with them. On one particular occasion when I came to minister to this businessman's staff, I noticed there was a new girl at the receptionist's desk—a young Asian lady. So, I asked her why she wasn't in with the other employees for the meeting. She said since she was the new person, she had to stay and answer the phones. Then she asked me if I was the one who was going to speak, and I said, "Yes."

She asked what I did, and I told her I was a minister. She asked, "For whom?"

I said, "Well, for the Lord Jesus Christ."

Then she exclaimed, "You're the one!"

I said, "The one what?"

She proceeded to tell me that as she was going through her rituals the previous night (she was either Hindu or Buddhist), she started doubting that her god was the true God. She stopped in the middle of her ritual and said, "God, I know You exist, but there's got to be more to You than this. Would you please reveal Yourself to me, and let me know who the true God is?"

As soon as she prayed this, a ball of light came right up to her, and she heard a voice say, "I will send you a man tomorrow who will tell you who I am."

Then she looked at me and said, "You're the one!"

I said, "I am the one. Amen."

I had the opportunity to lead her to the Lord, and she was baptized in the Holy Ghost and spoke with tongues. When I got back to my car, I had such a sense of peace and joy from knowing that I was at the right place at the right time. There was such satisfaction knowing that I was exactly where I was supposed to be. Some of you have never experienced this because you are not where you are supposed to be. You are taking the safe route. You're shooting at nothing and hitting it every time. You've been taught that you have to be logical and do things according to the way everyone else in your family has done it. But you are limiting God!

COMPARING YOURSELVES AMONG YOURSELVES

For we dare not make ourselves of the number, or compare ourselves with some that commend themselves: but they measuring themselves by themselves, and comparing themselves among themselves, are not wise.

2 CORINTHIANS 10:12, EMPHASIS MINE

Most people limit God by comparing themselves with others, yet it is so clear in Scripture that we should not measure ourselves by other people. Instead of letting the Word of God control and dominate our thoughts, we look at our parents, our grandparents, and the television, and we listen to people's experiences about all the bad things that have happened to them. Then we start expecting these things to happen to us and limit God by comparing ourselves among ourselves. One area in which we do this is finances. We look around and see that there's a recession, so we expect this to happen to us.

In Colorado Springs there are hundreds of parachurch ministries, and when the "recession" occurred in 2008, many of these ministries decreased their revenue projections by 15 to 25 percent—before a single decrease in revenue ever happened. They anticipated it because the world was having problems, and they began planning for it and expecting it to happen to them. And guess what? It came to pass.

During that exact time, our finances flourished! We began a $60 million building program in the fall of 2009—a program we were going to complete debt free—and our ministry finances were going up like a rocket during the recession. We just decided not to participate in the recession, so we didn't anticipate it and plan for it. As a result, we never experienced it in our ministry.

But my God shall supply all your need according to his riches in glory by Christ Jesus.
PHILIPPIANS 4:19

Finances don't have to be dictated by the world. They can be dictated by heaven's economy, not this world's system. Several years ago, Jamie's father left her an inheritance, which we invested in the stock market. When the stock market went down at the end of 2008 and the beginning of 2009 by 50 percent, we increased our investment by 61 percent. That's a 61 percent increase during a 50 percent downturn! God blessed us! Our investor couldn't even understand why we were prospering so much. Some are too carnal to believe that's true, thinking there's a natural reason. No, it's the blessing of God. Our investor told us that his other clients didn't prosper as much as we did. It's because we were believing God. As a man thinks in his heart, so is he (Prov. 23:7)—and we were bucking the trend. Some look to the economy and start cutting back, not expecting to prosper. This limits what God can do.

Some of you cut back on your giving during those times because you anticipate having a problem, but you should cut back on your debt and your spending—not your giving! The worst thing you can do to limit your harvest is cut back on your sowing. If anything, you need to increase your giving! But most people don't think this way, so they limit God.

Before the Lord spoke to me in 2002, I thought I was truly believing Him—*compared* to where I had been and *compared* to others, I thought I was doing good. And I was doing good *compared* to other people, but it's not wise to compare yourself with others. It doesn't matter if everyone in your family has always been a loser. That doesn't dictate what will happen to you, unless you believe it's in your genes to be a loser. Just because everyone else is suffering in the economy doesn't mean you have to suffer, unless you believe you have to suffer. Comparing yourselves among yourselves and measuring yourselves by the world is the wrong measurement.

If you listen to the news for just a few minutes, you will hear a lot of junk. There's so much negativity on the news. For instance, they will talk about flu season and everyone getting their flu shots. Most people think, *I'm only human. I'll get the flu if I don't get those shots.* If you listen to everyone and think you are going to get the flu, you will. But there is no season when the Word of God doesn't work—not even the flu season. You need to stand on scriptures like Psalm 91 and declare that no plague will come near your dwelling. I'm determined to stand on the Word of God and walk in supernatural health.

Most of us listen to the sewage of this world and hear what the world is experiencing, so we expect to get sick. We let what happens in the world affect us. We may say, "Oh, I'm only human." But if we're born again, we are not *only* human: One-third of us is wall-to-wall Holy Ghost—one-third of us is saved (i.e., the spirit). We should not get the same stuff the world gets. We shouldn't be comparing ourselves with those who don't have God living on the inside of them. That's ignorance. The politically correct way to say this is that it's our lack of knowledge that's the problem. In Texas, we would say, "You're stupid. How dumb can you get and still breathe?"

My dad died when he was fifty-four. He was a functional invalid my entire life. He could never throw a ball or do anything active with me. When I was twelve years old, he died from heart problems. People said that I was going to have heart problems, hardening of the arteries, high blood pressure, and all kinds of other problems when I got older, since these things are hereditary. But one of the first things I did when I got turned on to the Lord was to cancel that curse—I broke it. It didn't matter what happened to my dad. It wasn't going to happen to me.

My mother, on the other hand, lived to be ninety-six and was as strong as a horse until her final years. Why didn't people tell me that the good genes of my mother would help me, instead of only focusing on the bad genes of my dad and pronouncing the worst possible outcome over me? It's because people tend to look at the worst-case scenario. Most people will say, "Well, my dad had heart problems, so I guess I'll have heart problems." They just accept these things as fact. They need to stop comparing themselves with their parents and other people. This thinking limits the healing God wants to do in their bodies.

Most people do not let the Word of God get in the way of what they believe. They think that's the way it's always been in their families, so that's the way it's going to be. They need to change the way they believe. Many of them believe like this in so many subtle ways that they don't even recognize it. For instance, a lot of ladies have been taught that for two to six days of the month they are justified in acting like the devil. God didn't create women to be that way, but they have bought into an ungodly standard. If they believe that's the way it has to be, Satan will accommodate them.

Jamie used to have "female" problems when she was young, but she believed God for healing and overcame all of that. She went through menopause and didn't fall apart like a $2 suitcase or have to take hormone replacement therapy or anything else. She walked through this season supernaturally. Yet many women believe that menopause has to be miserable and that they have to experience all of its symptoms—but who says so? They have been trained in the natural way, so they accept living at a lower standard, believing that they have to get sick, get the flu, or get headaches, or that they can't live without any pain.

I don't have any pain in my body, and I'm over sixty years old. I've been sick one time in forty-plus years, and that was due to my own stupidity. I had ministered forty-one times in one week and forty-two times the next week, and I became so tired, I literally had to crawl into bed. I stayed in bed one day to recuperate and then went out the next day to cut a cord of wood. It was too much, too soon, and I got sick. You can chalk that up to stupidity! That's the only time I've been sick. I don't believe in getting sick. I don't take sickness. Some of you think you can't live that way, but don't wake me up because that's the way I'm living. When you expect sickness, you limit God.

If you are sick, you don't have to find out everything about your sickness. Don't focus on the sickness; focus on what God's Word says. His Word says that all things are possible to them who believe. You should be speaking the Word to yourself concerning healing. Put scriptures somewhere that you can see them often and focus on them. But instead of focusing on God's Word, a lot of people limit God by being plugged into the world and being concerned about what's going on in everyone else's lives.

LESSON 1.2 • WRONG BELIEFS
OUTLINE

VII. Many of us use Ephesians 3:20 to say that God is able to do anything, but it's *"according to the power that worketh in us"*—

Now unto him that is able to do exceeding abundantly above all that we ask or think, according to the power that worketh in us.

   A. If we are not building ourselves up on our most holy faith (Jude 20), then we limit the power of God that flows from us.
   B. If we're not healed, it's not God who didn't heal us—it's us not releasing the power of God on the inside of us.
   C. When we say that God just sovereignly moved, we are saying that no person had anything to do with His moving.
   D. That is not scriptural, because God always uses people.

VIII. God doesn't move in waves.
   A. That's not the way God operates; He wants every single one of us to walk in His fullness.
   B. He would pour out movements all at one time if we would receive them that way.
   C. If we'll stop limiting Him, He *can* do what He's always wanted.

IX. God wants to move and bring us into our Promised Land.
   A. He has a purpose for us, and when we find it, we will be fulfilled.
   B. Some of us have never experienced this because we are not where we are supposed to be—we are taking the safe route.
   C. We've been taught to be logical and do things according to the way everyone else in our families has done it, but we are limiting God!

X. It is so clear in Scripture that we should not measure ourselves by ourselves or the world.

For we dare not make ourselves *of the number, or* compare ourselves *with some that* commend themselves: *but they measuring themselves by themselves, and comparing themselves among themselves, are not wise.*

2 CORINTHIANS 10:12, EMPHASIS MINE

A. Instead we should let the Word of God control and dominate our thoughts.

B. Many of us look at our parents, grandparents, or the television, and we listen to all the bad things that have happened to other people.

C. We start expecting these things to happen to us and limit God by comparing ourselves among ourselves.

D. We look around and see that there's a recession, so we expect this to happen to us.

But my God shall supply all your need according to his riches in glory by Christ Jesus.
PHILIPPIANS 4:19

E. Many of us let what happens in the world affect us.

    i. We may say "Oh, I'm only human," but if we're born again, we are not *only* human: One-third of us (i.e., the spirit) is wall-to-wall Holy Ghost.

F. We shouldn't limit God by being plugged into the world and concerned about what's going on in everyone else's lives.

LESSON 1.2 • WRONG BELIEFS
TEACHER'S GUIDE

7.   Many of us use Ephesians 3:20 to say that God is able to do anything, but it's *"according to the power that worketh in us"*—

> *Now unto him that is able to do exceeding abundantly above all that we ask or think, according to the power that worketh in us.*

If we are not building ourselves up on our most holy faith (Jude 20), then we limit the power of God that flows from us. If we're not healed, it's not God who didn't heal us—it's us not releasing the power of God on the inside of us. When we say that God just sovereignly moved, we are saying that no person had anything to do with His moving. That is not scriptural, because God always uses people.

7a.   Not building yourself up on your most _____ _____ limits the power of God that flows through you.
       Holy faith
7b.   If you are not healed, it's because _____.
       A. God did not heal you
       B. You don't want to be healed
       C. You are not releasing the power in you
       D. All of the above
       E. None of the above
       C. You are not releasing the power in you
7c.   *Discussion question:* Why is it not scriptural to say that God sovereignly moves?
       Discussion question

8.   God doesn't move in waves. That's not the way God operates; He wants every single one of us to walk in His fullness. He would pour out movements all at one time if we would receive them that way. If we'll stop limiting Him, He *can* do what He's always wanted.

8a.   True or false: God moves in waves.
       False
8b.   God wants you to _____ in His _____.
       Walk / fullness
8c.   *Discussion question:* What movements of God do you think would happen if people stopped limiting Him?
       Discussion question

9.   God wants to move and bring us into our Promised Land. He has a purpose for us, and when we find it, we will be fulfilled. Some of us have never experienced this because we are not where we are supposed to be—we are taking the safe route. We've been taught to be logical and do things according to the way everyone else in our families has done it, but we are limiting God!

9a.   What happens when you find God's purpose for you?
      You will be fulfilled

9b.   What is one reason you may not be where you're supposed to be?
      A.   You are taking the safe route
      B.   You don't have a navigation system in your car
      C.   You haven't listened to enough of Andrew's teachings
      D.   A and B
      E.   A and C
      A.   You are taking the safe route

9c.   *Discussion question:* How do logic and family traditions limit God?
      Discussion question

10. It is so clear in Scripture that we should not measure ourselves by ourselves or the world.

> *For we dare not make* ourselves *of the number, or* compare ourselves *with some that commend themselves: but they measuring themselves by themselves, and comparing themselves among themselves, are not wise.*
> 2 CORINTHIANS 10:12, EMPHASIS MINE

Instead we should let the Word of God control and dominate our thoughts. Many of us look at our parents, grandparents, or the television, and we listen to all the bad things that have happened to other people. We start expecting these things to happen to us and limit God by comparing ourselves among ourselves. We look around and see that there's a recession, so we expect this to happen to us.

> *But my God shall supply all your need according to his riches in glory by Christ Jesus.*
> PHILIPPIANS 4:19

Many of us let what happens in the world affect us. We may say "Oh, I'm only human," but if we're born again, we are not *only* human: One-third of us (i.e., the spirit) is wall-to-wall Holy Ghost. We shouldn't limit God by being plugged into the world and concerned about what's going on in everyone else's lives.

10a. What should you allow to control and dominate your thoughts?
   A. The Word of God
   B. The news on television
   C. The recommendations of doctors
   D. All of the above
   E. None of the above
   A. The Word of God
10b. Why do many start expecting bad things to happen?
   They compare themselves among themselves
10c. True or false: If you're born again, you're only human.
   False
10d. *Discussion question:* How can being plugged into the world and being concerned about what's going on in everyone else's lives limit God?
   Discussion question

LESSON 1.2 • WRONG BELIEFS
DISCIPLESHIP QUESTIONS

21. Not building yourself up on your most _____ _____ limits the power of God that flows through you.

22. If you are not healed, it's because _____.
    A. God did not heal you
    B. You don't want to be healed
    C. You are not releasing the power in you
    D. All of the above
    E. None of the above

23. *Discussion question:* Why is it not scriptural to say that God sovereignly moves?

    _____
    _____
    _____

24. True or false: God moves in waves.

25. God wants you to _____ in His _____.

26. *Discussion question:* What movements of God do you think would happen if people stopped limiting Him?

    _____
    _____
    _____

27. What happens when you find God's purpose for you?

    _____
    _____
    _____

28. What is one reason you may not be where you're supposed to be?
    A. You are taking the safe route
    B. You don't have a navigation system in your car
    C. You haven't listened to enough of Andrew's teachings
    D. A and B
    E. A and C

29. *Discussion question:* How do logic and family traditions limit God?

    _____
    _____
    _____

30. What should you allow to control and dominate your thoughts?
    A. The Word of God
    B. The news on television
    C. The recommendations of doctors
    D. All of the above
    E. None of the above

31. Why do many start expecting bad things to happen?

    _____
    _____
    _____

32. True or false: If you're born again, you're only human.

33. *Discussion question:* How can being plugged into the world and being concerned about what's going on in everyone else's lives limit God?

    _____
    _____
    _____

LESSON 1.2 • WRONG BELIEFS
ANSWER KEY

21. Holy faith
22. C. You are not releasing the power in you
23. *Discussion question*
24. False
25. Walk / fullness
26. *Discussion question*
27. You will be fulfilled
28. A. You are taking the safe route
29. *Discussion question*
30. A. The Word of God
31. They compare themselves among themselves
32. False
33. *Discussion question*

LESSON 1.2 • WRONG BELIEFS

SCRIPTURES

EPHESIANS 3:20

Now unto him that is able to do exceeding abundantly above all that we ask or think, according to the power that worketh in us.

JUDE 20

But ye, beloved, building up yourselves on your most holy faith, praying in the Holy Ghost.

2 CORINTHIANS 10:12

For we dare not make ourselves of the number, or compare ourselves with some that commend themselves: but they measuring themselves by themselves, and comparing themselves among themselves, are not wise.

PHILIPPIANS 4:19

But my God shall supply all your need according to his riches in glory by Christ Jesus.

PROVERBS 23:7

For as he thinketh in his heart, so is he: Eat and drink, saith he to thee; but his heart is not with thee.

WRONG BELIEFS

There should be a difference between Christians and those who don't know God. Believers are alive, and non-believers are dead. There's a difference between a corpse and someone who's alive. Some Christians are as sick as their neighbors, as poor as their neighbors, as depressed as their neighbors, and as negative as their neighbors, who don't even know God. If some Christians were arrested for being Christians, there wouldn't even be enough evidence to convict them. There ought to be a difference. God made everyone for more than what they are experiencing in their lives. God made Christians for more than average. If they are average, that means they aren't good or bad; they are lukewarm (Rev. 3:16). God made every Christian special. If they aren't feeling that way, they need to take the limits off God.

This is not only true in health, finances, and the things happening in this world, but it's also true in the spiritual realm. Most people aren't truly seeking God and listening to Him. They do not have a close relationship with Him, so they start thinking, *Well, most people don't see things come to pass, so it's okay for me not to see total victory either.* They limit God by the way they think.

An example of this is what happened after the 9/11 terrorist attacks. The income for most ministries decreased anywhere from 25 to 40 percent after September 11, 2001, because everyone's attention was focused on the attacks. People stopped watching television and listening to the radio, except to view or hear about the events of 9/11 and its aftermath. Everyone was trying to figure out what was going on. People were mostly giving to the Red Cross and other similar organizations.

Most major ministries were on the verge of going under during that time. But since 9/11, our ministry's income has tripled. It increased substantially! Immediately after 9/11, we were increasing. We even had months with record-setting income! If this worked for us, it could have worked for everyone.

God is no respecter of persons (Rom. 2:11). Believers should be doing better than the average person. After all, Jesus died to deliver us from this present evil world (Gal. 1:4). But sadly, that is not every believer's experience.

Are you limiting what God wants to do for you or through you by comparing yourself with others? Do you really want to just be like everyone else with the same diseases and the same financial and emotional problems? You need to go to the Word and find out what it says. God's Word will make you far, far, far above, and not beneath.

> *And the LORD shall make thee the head, and not the tail; and thou shalt be above only, and thou shalt not be beneath; if that thou hearken unto the commandments of the LORD thy God, which I command thee this day, to observe and to do them.*
>
> DEUTERONOMY 28:13

If we ask people how they're doing, they might say, "Well, pretty good under the circumstances." We need to tell them to get out from under there! We are supposed to be above only and not beneath. We're the head and not the tail. We're supposed to be rejoicing in the midst of problems. There are no excuses, but there are reasons we have problems. I'm not condemning anyone, and I'm not saying we live in a perfect world where everything is going to always be rosy; but I am saying that God did not create anyone for failure. If we are experiencing failure, He doesn't want us to live that way. God loves us. He wants us to win. He created us to be winners. We are winners!

YOU CAN DO IT

When the Lord spoke to me and told me that I was limiting Him, I called my staff together. I told them that I didn't know how long it would take for me to change the image I had on the inside, but I knew I had limited God. I had not seen myself doing what God told me to do. I had told some people what God had spoken to me, but I couldn't see it.

I said, "I don't know how long it takes to change this image on the inside. It may take a week, a month, a year, or ten years—but I will change. I will do what God called me to do." I honestly didn't have a clue how long it would take. Within one week, my whole life was turned right-side up.

I had been trying to get on the second-largest television network in the nation for two years. I had been on this network over five times as a guest (I was allowed to preach for forty-five minutes at a time), and I was even friends with the people who ran it. Yet every time I tried to get on their network as a regular programmer, I was given a price that was double their rate card. My media buyer also tried to get me on, but it seemed like the network didn't want me on there. It didn't make sense why I couldn't get on this network when I was personal friends with those who ran it.

But within two days of telling my staff that I made the decision to change the image on the inside of me, I got a letter from my friend asking why I wasn't on his network. He said he didn't know what the problem was but that I could plan on starting my programming on Monday and that they would work out the financial details later. Within one week, I was on that network, and our television outreach increased tremendously.

In another situation, Jamie and I had been praying for someone to help us with the ministry, because Jamie had been running the ministry as an administrator. She was doing a good job, but it was not her forte. Our ministry was growing beyond us, so we needed help. But would we find someone who had our heart for the ministry and who would let us give our products away? We've given away tens of millions of tapes, books, CDs, DVDs, and other materials free of charge. Every person who helped us run our ministry told me that I was crazy, especially when they saw our finances and how we were struggling. They'd say, "Sell your stuff. Quit giving everything away." So, Jamie just took it over and ran it, because she had my heart. We agreed that this was what God told us to do.

A few days after I told my staff about my decision, I called one of our board members to cancel a board meeting. He told me that he was so glad I called because he and his wife had decided to take an early retirement, and they wanted to come to Colorado to help take the ministry to the next level. To make a long story short, he came to work for my ministry. I couldn't believe that someone who had my heart for the ministry, with his extensive background and expertise, would work for me. My ministry was small, and the income was pitiful. Yet he took an early retirement to come and help me.

When I made that decision in my heart to change and stop limiting God, instantly our television ministry tripled and God started bringing in the best people to help us. Then it took me two months to send a letter to our partners, telling them what God had spoken to my heart about limiting Him. It took another month for them to respond to my letter. So, it was three months total before people heard this from me. But before that, within a week or two, our income began to explode. Nobody knew anything! They didn't respond to me. There is something that happens in the spiritual realm when you start believing God. You've got to see God's purpose for your life and take the limits off Him. Believe He has something more for you than you are experiencing in your life.

When I took the limits off God and started doing what He called me to do, our ministry took off. Over the next twelve years, our incoming phone calls increased by about 1,500 percent. Now, over 1.1 million visit my website per month—roughly 37,000 visits a day. My ministry employs over 300 people (up from 30 in 2001), and online orders have increased by about 5,000 percent. The ministry's revenue (not including revenue for the Bible colleges and foreign offices) has increased from about $2.2 million in 2001 to $38 million in 2013. That is a big increase! We are building a $65 million campus, with the first $32 million-phase completed in January 2014 and paid for debt free.

This is phenomenal. This is rare! God is multiplying us in every direction we turn. **And the best is yet to come!**

It all started when God told me I was limiting Him with my small thinking. When I changed my thinking and started believing differently, I saw the supernatural power of God. Many of you want these results as you read this book but are hesitant to receive the spark that caused this explosion in my life. But you can't have the fruit without the root.

You can take the limits off God! You can start to see God multiply and increase your effectiveness and transform your life. And it doesn't have to take ten years. It could start within a week or two if you get your thinking straight. It might take longer for the manifestation to come. A lot of things God began to do in my life were still taking place five or ten years later. But once you make this adjustment in your heart, it's just a matter of time until you see the results in your life.

I haven't arrived, but I have left. I'm on my way. Some of you haven't left. Some of you are stuck. Some of you want things to be different, but if you don't change some of the ways you are thinking, you will be back next year in the exact same spot, praying and asking God to do the same things. It's not God who is limiting Himself—it's you! You are limiting Him by your stinking thinking, and you are going to have to change the way you think. You're going to have to quit comparing yourself to others. You're going to have to get in the Word, find people who did the extraordinary, and say that God's no respecter of persons—if He did it for them, He will do it for you (Acts 10:34). Let the Word of God challenge you. Let the Holy Spirit speak through you and paint a picture of who you're supposed to be and what you're supposed to be doing. Start taking the limits off God!

LESSON 1.3 • WRONG BELIEFS
OUTLINE

XI.   There should be a difference between Christians and those who don't know God.
- A. God made believers for more than what they are experiencing in their lives—He made them for more than average.
- B. If they are average, that means they aren't good or bad; they are lukewarm (Rev. 3:16).
- C. This is not only true in health, finances, and the things happening in this world, but it's also true in the spiritual realm.
- D. Most people aren't truly seeking God and listening to Him.
- E. They do not have a close relationship with Him, so they start thinking, *Well, most people don't see things come to pass, so it's okay for me not to see total victory either.*
- F. They limit God by the way they think.

XII. We as believers should be doing better than the average person.
- A. After all, Jesus died to deliver us from this present evil world (Gal. 1:4).
- B. But sadly, that is not every believer's experience.
- C. Do we really want to just be like everyone else with the same diseases and the same financial and emotional problems?
- D. God's Word will make us far, far, far above, and not beneath (Deut. 28:13).
  - i.   We're the head and not the tail.
  - ii. We're supposed to be rejoicing in the midst of problems.
  - iii. God did not create anyone for failure—He created us to be winners!

XIII. There is something that happens in the spiritual realm when you start believing God.
- A. You've got to see God's purpose for your life and take the limits off Him.
- B. Believe He has something more for you than you are experiencing in your life.
- C. When I changed my thinking and started believing differently, I saw the supernatural power of God.
- D. But you can't have the fruit without the root.

XIV. You can take the limits off God!
- A. You can start to see God multiply and increase your effectiveness and transform your life.
- B. Once you make this adjustment in your heart, it's just a matter of time until you see the results in your life.
- C. Let the Word of God challenge you.

D. Let the Holy Spirit speak through you and paint a picture of who you're supposed to be and what you're supposed to be doing.

LESSON 1.3 • WRONG BELIEFS
TEACHER'S GUIDE

11.   There should be a difference between us Christians and those who don't know God. God made us for more than what we are experiencing in our lives—He made us for more than average. If we are average, that means we aren't good or bad; we are lukewarm (Rev. 3:16). This is not only true in our health, our finances, and in the things that are happening in this world, but it's also true in the spiritual realm. Most of us aren't truly seeking God and listening to Him. If we do not have a close relationship with Him, we start thinking, *Well, most people don't see things come to pass, so it's okay for me not to see total victory either.* We limit God by the way we think.

11a.   True or false: There should be a difference between Christians and those who don't know God.
True

11b.   *Discussion question:* Read Revelation 3:16. What is the danger of being lukewarm?
Discussion question

11c.   Most people aren't truly _____ God and _____ to Him.
Seeking / listening

11d.   If you don't have a close relationship with God, you might think, _____.
    A. *It's okay for me not to see total victory*
    B. *Most people don't see things come to pass*
    C. *God no longer answers prayers*
    D. B and C
    E. A and B
    E. A and B

12.   We as believers should be doing better than the average person. After all, Jesus died to deliver us from this present evil world (Gal. 1:4). But sadly, that is not every believer's experience. Do we really want to just be like everyone else with the same diseases and the same financial and emotional problems? God's Word will make us far, far, far above, and not beneath (Deut. 28:13). We're the head and not the tail. We're supposed to be rejoicing in the midst of problems. God did not create anyone for failure—He created us to be winners!

12a.   *Discussion question:* Why doesn't every believer do better than the average person, who isn't delivered from this present evil world?
Discussion question

12b.   What will make you far above the diseases and financial and emotional problems of people in the world?
The Word

12c.   God did not create anyone for _____.
Failure

---

13. There is something that happens in the spiritual realm when we start believing God. We've got to see God's purpose for our lives and take the limits off Him. We need to believe He has something more for us than we are experiencing in our lives. When Andrew changed his thinking and started believing differently, he saw the supernatural power of God. But we can't have the fruit without the root.

13a. When you start believing God, where will things begin to happen?
In the spiritual realm

14. We can take the limits off God! We can start to see God multiply and increase our effectiveness and transform our lives. Once we make this adjustment in our hearts, it's just a matter of time until we see the results in our lives. Let's let the Word of God challenge us. Let's let the Holy Spirit speak through us and paint a picture of who we're supposed to be and what we're supposed to be doing.

14a. When you take the limits off God, what will you start to see?
  A. God increase your effectiveness
  B. God transform your life
  C. A picture of what you're supposed to be
  D. A picture of what you're supposed to be doing
  E. All of the above
  E. All of the above

14b. If you make this adjustment in _____ _____, it's just a matter of time until you see the results.
Your heart

LESSON 1.3 • WRONG BELIEFS
DISCIPLESHIP QUESTIONS

34. True or false: There should be a difference between Christians and those who don't know God.

35. *Discussion question:* Read Revelation 3:16. What is the danger of being lukewarm?

   _____

   _____

   _____

36. Most people aren't truly _____ God and _____ to Him.

37. If you don't have a close relationship with God, you might think, _____.
   A. *It's okay for me not to see total victory*
   B. *Most people don't see things come to pass*
   C. *God no longer answers prayers*
   D. B and C
   E. A and B

38. *Discussion question:* Why doesn't every believer do better than the average person, who isn't delivered from this present evil world?

   _____

   _____

   _____

39. What will make you far above the diseases and financial and emotional problems of people in the world?

   _____

   _____

   _____

40. God did not create anyone for _____.

41. When you start believing God, where will things begin to happen?

   _____

   _____

   _____

42. When you take the limits off God, what will you start to see?
   A. God increase your effectiveness
   B. God transform your life
   C. A picture of what you're supposed to be
   D. A picture of what you're supposed to be doing
   E. All of the above

43. If you make this adjustment in _____ _____, it's just a matter of time until you see the results.

LESSON 1.3 • WRONG BELIEFS
ANSWER KEY

34. True
35. *Discussion question*
36. Seeking / listening
37. E. A and B
38. *Discussion question*
39. The Word
40. Failure
41. In the spiritual realm
42. E. All of the above
43. Your heart

LESSON 1.3 • WRONG BELIEFS

SCRIPTURES

REVELATION 3:16

So then because thou art lukewarm, and neither cold nor hot, I will spue thee out of my mouth.

ROMANS 2:11

For there is no respect of persons with God.

GALATIANS 1:4

Who gave himself for our sins, that he might deliver us from this present evil world, according to the will of God and our Father.

DEUTERONOMY 28:13

And the LORD shall make thee the head, and not the tail; and thou shalt be above only, and thou shalt not be beneath; if that thou hearken unto the commandments of the LORD thy God, which I command thee this day, to observe and to do them.

ACTS 10:34

Then Peter opened his mouth, and said, Of a truth I perceive that God is no respecter of persons.

CARES OF THIS WORLD

It is easy nowadays to let the cares of this world, the deceitfulness of riches, and the lusts of other things enter in and choke the Word. These distractions limit God and keep us from understanding His plan for our lives.

And these are they which are sown among thorns; such as hear the word, [19] And the cares of this world, and the deceitfulness of riches, and the lusts of other things entering in, choke the word, and it becometh unfruitful.

MARK 4:18-19

When the seed (the Word of God) is planted in the ground (our hearts), it has the potential to produce a hundredfold. But the seed doesn't determine how much is produced; the ground does. If we have so many thorns in our lives and allow the cares of this world, the deceitfulness of riches, and the lusts of other things enter into our hearts and choke God's Word, then we limit what He can do in our lives.

BE STILL

We cannot really understand the greatness of God without being still and shutting some things out. We need to be quiet and let Him speak to us. Psalm 46:10 says, *"Be still, and know that I am God."* When Jamie and I were in Washington, D.C., the week President Reagan died, we had the opportunity to attend his funeral procession. As we walked down the National Mall on a gravel path, I noticed that we couldn't hear a single sound from our footsteps on the gravel. There was no one around talking or making any noise, yet we could not hear the gravel as we walked.

The next day we went to Shenandoah National Park, and we walked on a gravel path on the Appalachian Trail. There, the sound of our footsteps on the gravel was so loud it echoed through the forest. I wondered how we could hear our footsteps on the gravel there but not when we were at the

National Mall the day before. The Lord spoke to me and said it was because of all the ambient noise in Washington, D.C.—the planes, the traffic, and all the other background noise. If we are busy and have too much going on in the background of our lives, we will limit our ability to hear God and will miss what He is telling us to do.

> *And he said, Go forth, and stand upon the mount before the LORD. And, behold, the LORD passed by, and a great and strong wind rent the mountains, and brake in pieces the rocks before the LORD; but the LORD was not in the wind: and after the wind an earthquake; but the LORD was not in the earthquake: [12] And after the earthquake a fire; but the LORD was not in the fire: and after the fire a still small voice.*
>
> 1 KINGS 19:11-12

Elijah witnessed an earthquake, a fire, and a mighty wind that was so strong, it destroyed the rocks. But God wasn't in any of those spectacular things; He simply spoke in a still, small voice. This is the number one way God speaks to us. He can yell and do things in a spectacular way, but the true nature of God is a still, small voice.

Jesus said, *"I am meek and lowly in heart: and ye shall find rest unto your souls"* (Matt. 11:29). When Jesus came to the earth, He could have come in a 747 and landed in Jerusalem. That would have attracted a lot of attention! But instead, He came and announced His arrival to shepherds.

The way that 99 percent of us are going to relate to the Lord is not through something dramatic like a blinding flash of light but, rather, through something subtle and simple. But if we're not careful, we will let the cares of this world, the deceitfulness of riches, and the lusts of other things enter in and cause us to miss that still, small voice. Psalm 46:10 tells us to *"be still, and know that I am God"*—we have to be still.

Most people's lifestyles are not conducive to having a relationship with God. They cram their lives full of "stuff" and never have any downtime. If they happen to have free time, they just plop in front of the television. They never have a time when their minds are free to be led by God. This limits what God can do in their lives.

Some years ago, I had a dream. In this dream, I saw a banner with "Psalm 46:10" on it, but for the life of me, I could not remember what that verse said. I've quoted that verse hundreds of times, but I couldn't remember what it said that day. When I woke up, I looked the scripture up: *"Be still, and know that I am God."*

I didn't know exactly what this scripture meant, but I thought, *Well, just in case, I'm gonna be still and not move.* So, for over an hour and a half, I sat out on my deck and never moved. Deer came up to me and stared me right in the face. Chipmunks came and sat on my feet and climbed up my legs. I watched thousands and thousands of ants crawl everywhere. I heard birds flying and the wind blowing.

I had not noticed these things before, but once I became still, I realized that this activity was going on around me constantly yet I would get so busy that I missed it. We are completely oblivious to these things because of our busy lifestyles. Likewise, in the spiritual realm, God is constantly speaking to us. Have you ever wondered how birds can fly thousands and thousands of miles and land at the exact same place, on the exact same day, every year? Or how fish know where to go to spawn every year? Psalm 19:1 says, *"The heavens declare the glory of God; and the firmament sheweth his handywork."*

Creation is shouting at us every single day. Every sunrise and sunset is a tremendous testimony of the awesomeness of God. God is constantly speaking to us, yet we are too busy to hear Him. Our lifestyles are choking what God wants to do in our lives. We need to spend time being still and letting God speak to us. But many people don't like to do this because when they get still, it's like there is a homing device or little beeper that goes off and they begin to think, *Is this all there is? Is this all my life is meant to be? Is there something more? Am I really doing what God called me to do?* Most people are uncomfortable with these questions and don't want to deal with them, so they drown them out. This keeps them from hearing the voice of God.

Our lifestyles are so busy that we often talk about how busy we are. If we have any extra time, we fill it with something. We multitask and brag about how we can do multiple things. Rather than boasting about our busyness, we need to get to a place in our lives that's conducive to hearing God's voice.

Jesus separated His disciples and told them to come apart and rest awhile (Mark 6:31). Jesus went into the desert to rest, but the crowds followed Him around the lake and wouldn't let Him rest. So, He stayed up all night praying (Matt. 14). Jesus was recharging His spiritual batteries by communing with His Father. This was more important to Him than sleep. If Jesus needed to separate—to come apart and rest awhile—and if Jesus told His disciples to rest awhile, then we need to follow His example and do the same.

YOU CHOOSE

O LORD, I know that the way of man is not in himself: it is not in man that walketh to direct his steps.

JEREMIAH 10:23

God has given us the authority to run our own lives. We're allowed to run our lives, but it's a wrong choice. We can only reach our full potential when we become God dependent and look to Him for leadership. God did not create us to run our own lives. *"The way of man is not in himself."* We need to spend time with God and His Word and follow His plan for our lives.

Let's take a look at this scripture in Deuteronomy:

> *I call heaven and earth to record this day against you, that I have set before you life and death, blessing and cursing: therefore choose life, that both thou and thy seed may live.*
>
> DEUTERONOMY 30:19

God gave us a choice, but He told us what choice to make. The right choice is to choose life—to choose God. We need to become responsive to God, yet we can't do that when the cares of this life and other things are choking the Word of God on the inside of us. It takes time and effort. People often say, "I don't have a large quantity of time, but I have quality time." But we need to spend *quantity* time with the Lord. We need to keep our minds stayed on Him. That doesn't mean we have to become preachers or stop working in the secular world. We can keep our minds stayed on the Lord regardless of what we do.

I wasn't always a preacher. I got drafted into the army. I was completely submerged in and surrounded by ungodliness, yet I kept my mind stayed on the Lord and put Him first in the midst of terrible situations. I've also worked secular jobs. I've poured concrete for a living, and I was able to keep my mind stayed on the Lord. You can do this too!

The part of you that meditates on the Word is the same part that worries. Worry is meditation in a negative form. Have you ever gone to work while you were worrying about your family, your finances, your health, or some other problem? Even though you were worrying, you could still function at your job. In the same way, you can keep your mind stayed upon the Lord.

> *(For the weapons of our warfare are not carnal, but mighty through God to the pulling down of strong holds;) [5] Casting down imaginations, and every high thing that exalteth itself against the knowledge of God, and bringing into captivity every thought to the obedience of Christ.*
>
> 2 CORINTHIANS 10:4-5

We have the power to bring every thought into captivity to the obedience of Christ. We can keep our minds stayed upon the Lord. Isaiah 26:3 says, *"Thou wilt keep him in perfect peace, whose mind is stayed on thee: because he trusteth in thee."* If we are not in perfect peace, our minds are not stayed on the Lord. We are listening to the same junk that the world is listening to, instead of listening to the Word of God.

If we are going to take the limits off God, we are going to have to diminish the ungodliness and all the junk of this world that is coming into our hearts, and we're going to have to still ourselves, be quiet, and start listening to God. We're going to have to start facing some of our hard questions: Is this all there is to life? Is this all that God wants us to do? Is there something more? Are we in the right professions? Is this what God led us to do? Until we start entertaining these thoughts and being still and letting God speak to us, we will continue to limit God. We will become like those who are up to their eyeballs in debt. We will get the same results as long as we do the same things that they do. We need to be still.

LESSON 2.1 • CARES OF THIS WORLD
OUTLINE

I.   It is easy nowadays to let the cares of this world, the deceitfulness of riches, and the lusts of other things enter in and choke the Word:

And these are they which are sown among thorns; such as hear the word, [19] And the cares of this world, and the deceitfulness of riches, and the lusts of other things entering in, choke the word, and it becometh unfruitful.

MARK 4:18-19

A.   When the seed (the Word of God) is planted in the ground (our hearts), it has the potential to produce a hundredfold.

B.   But the seed doesn't determine how much is produced; the ground does.

C.   When things enter into our hearts and choke God's Word, we limit what God can do in our lives.

II. We cannot really understand the greatness of God without being still and shutting some things out.

A.   Psalm 46:10 says, *"Be still, and know that I am God."*

B.   If we are busy and have too much going on in the background of our lives, we will limit our ability to hear God and will miss what He is telling us to do.

And he said, Go forth, and stand upon the mount before the LORD. And, behold, the LORD passed by, and a great and strong wind rent the mountains, and brake in pieces the rocks before the LORD; but the LORD was not in the wind: and after the wind an earthquake; but the LORD was not in the earthquake: [12] And after the earthquake a fire; but the LORD was not in the fire: and after the fire a still small voice.

1 KINGS 19:11-12

C.   God can yell and do things in a spectacular way, but the true nature of God is a still, small voice.

D.   Jesus said, *"I'm meek and lowly in heart, and ye shall find rest unto your souls"* (Matt. 11:29).

E.   The way that 99 percent of us are going to relate to the Lord is through something subtle and simple.

III. God is constantly speaking to us, but we need to spend time being still.
    A. Many of us don't like to be still, because when we do, we begin to think, *Is this all there is? Is this all my life is meant to be? Is there something more? Am I really doing what God called me to do?*
    B. Most of us are uncomfortable with these questions and don't want to deal with them, so we drown them out.
    C. This keeps us from hearing the voice of God.
    D. Rather than boasting about our busyness, we need to get to a place that's conducive to hearing God's voice.
    E. Jesus separated His disciples and told them to come apart and rest awhile (Mark 6:31).
    F. Jesus Himself stayed up all night praying (Matt. 14), recharging His spiritual batteries by communing with His Father.
    G. If Jesus needed to separate, then we need to follow His example and do the same.

IV. God has given us the authority to run our own lives, but we can only reach our full potential when become God dependent and look to Him for leadership.

> *O LORD, I know that the way of man is not in himself: it is not in man that walketh to direct his steps.*
>
> JEREMIAH 10:23

    A. We need to spend time with God and His Word and follow His plan for our lives.

> *I call heaven and earth to record this day against you, that I have set before you life and death, blessing and cursing: therefore choose life, that both thou and thy seed may live.*
>
> DEUTERONOMY 30:19

    B. God gave us a choice, but the right choice is to choose life—to choose God.

V. You need to keep your mind stayed on the Lord.
    A. The part of you that meditates on the Word is the same part that worries.
    B. Worry is meditation in a negative form.
    C. You have the power to bring every thought into captivity to the obedience of Christ:

> *(For the weapons of our warfare are not carnal, but mighty through God to the pulling down of strong holds;) [5] Casting down imaginations, and every high thing that exalteth itself against the knowledge of God, and bringing into captivity every thought to the obedience of Christ.*
>
> 2 CORINTHIANS 10:4-5

D. If you are not in perfect peace, your mind is not stayed on the Lord (Is. 26:3).

E. If you are going to take the limits off God, you are going to have to diminish the junk of this world that is coming into your heart, still yourself, be quiet, and start listening to God.

LESSON 2.1 • CARES OF THIS WORLD
TEACHER'S GUIDE

1.   It is easy nowadays to let the cares of this world, the deceitfulness of riches, and the lusts of other things enter in and choke the Word:

> *And these are they which are sown among thorns; such as hear the word, [19] And the cares of this world, and the deceitfulness of riches, and the lusts of other things entering in, choke the word, and it becometh unfruitful.*
>
> MARK 4:18-19

When the seed (the Word of God) is planted in the ground (our hearts), it has the potential to produce a hundredfold. But the seed doesn't determine how much is produced; the ground does. When things enter into our hearts and choke God's Word, we limit what God can do in our lives.

1a.   According to Mark 4:18-19, what can happen when things of this world choke out the Word of God?
   A.   You can't have children
   B.   The Word becomes unfruitful
   C.   You can lose your job
   D.   All of the above
   E.   None of the above
   B.   The Word becomes unfruitful

1b.   *Discussion question:* What are some things that choke the Word and limit what God can do in your life?
   Discussion question

2.   We cannot really understand the greatness of God without being still and shutting some things out. Psalm 46:10 says, *"Be still, and know that I am God."* If we are busy and have too much going on in the background of our lives, we will limit our ability to hear God and will miss what He is telling us to do.

> *And he said, Go forth, and stand upon the mount before the* LORD. *And, behold, the* LORD *passed by, and a great and strong wind rent the mountains, and brake in pieces the rocks before the* LORD; *but the* LORD *was not in the wind: and after the wind an earthquake; but the* LORD *was not in the earthquake:* [12] *And after the earthquake a fire; but the* LORD *was not in the fire: and after the fire a still small voice.*
>
> 1 KINGS 19:11-12

God can yell and do things in a spectacular way, but the true nature of God is a still, small voice. Jesus said, *"I'm meek and lowly in heart, and ye shall find rest unto your souls"* (Matt. 11:29). The way that 99 percent of us are going to relate to the Lord is through something subtle and simple.

2a.   Psalm 46:10 says, *"Be* _____, *and* _____ *that I am God."*
      Still / know
2b.   If you are busy and have too much going on in the background of your life, what will happen?
      You will limit your ability to hear God and will miss what He is telling you to do
2c.   What did Jesus say in Matthew 11:29?
      A.   "I am the Son of God"
      B.   "I am proud and arrogant in heart"
      C.   "My yoke is easy and My burden is light"
      D.   "I am mighty and awesome, and here is a fireworks display"
      E.   "I am meek and lowly in heart"
      E.   "I am meek and lowly in heart"
2d.   *Discussion question:* Why do you think the main way you are going to relate to the Lord is through something subtle and simple?
      Discussion question

3.   God is constantly speaking to us, but we need to spend time being still. Many of us don't like to be still, because when we do, we begin to think, *Is this all there is? Is this all my life is meant to be? Is there something more? Am I really doing what God called me to do?* Most of us are uncomfortable with these questions and don't want to deal with them, so we drown them out. This keeps us from hearing the voice of God. Rather than boasting about our busyness, we need to get to a place that's conducive to hearing God's voice. Jesus separated His disciples and told them to come apart and rest awhile (Mark 6:31). Jesus Himself stayed up all night praying (Matt. 14), recharging His spiritual batteries by communing with His Father. If Jesus needed to separate, then we need to follow His example and do the same.

3a.   How often is God speaking to you?
        Constantly
3b.   Why do many not like to be still?
        A. They begin to think of questions that make them uncomfortable
        B. They hear strange noises
        C. They get telephone calls and need to talk
        D. All of the above
        E. None of the above
        A. They begin to think of questions that make them uncomfortable
3c.   *Discussion question:* Why do you think people tend to drown out uncomfortable questions and God's voice with busyness?
        Discussion question
3d.   What did Jesus have to do to recharge His spiritual batteries?
        A. Go on vacation
        B. Exercise His authority and demand His rest
        C. Stay up and commune with His Father
        D. All of the above
        E. None of the above
        C. Stay up and commune with His Father
3e.   If Jesus needed to separate, do you need to follow His example and do the same?
        Yes

4.   God has given us the authority to run our own lives, but we can only reach our full potential when we become God dependent and look to Him for leadership.

> *O Lord, I know that the way of man is not in himself: it is not in man that walketh to direct his steps.*
>
> JEREMIAH 10:23

We need to spend time with God and His Word and follow His plan for our lives.

> *I call heaven and earth to record this day against you, that I have set before you life and death, blessing and cursing: therefore choose life, that both thou and thy seed may live.*
>
> DEUTERONOMY 30:19

God gave us a choice, but the right choice is to choose life—to choose God.

4a.   Your full potential is reached when you become _____ _____, not independent.
God dependent

4b.   *Discussion question:* Why do you think God gave you a choice and told you to choose life (Deut. 30:19)?
Discussion question

5.   We need to keep our minds stayed on the Lord. The part of us that meditates on the Word is the same part that worries. Worry is meditation in a negative form. We have the power to bring every thought into captivity to the obedience of Christ:

> *(For the weapons of our warfare are not carnal, but mighty through God to the pulling down of strong holds;) [5] Casting down imaginations, and every high thing that exalteth itself against the knowledge of God, and bringing into captivity every thought to the obedience of Christ.*
>
> 2 CORINTHIANS 10:4-5

If we are not in perfect peace, our minds are not stayed on the Lord (Is. 26:3). If we are going to take the limits off God, we are going to have to diminish the junk of this world that is coming into our hearts, still ourselves, be quiet, and start listening to God.

5a.   True or false: Worry is meditation in a negative form.
True

5b.   According to 2 Corinthians 10:4-5, what do you have the power to do?
Bring every thought into captivity to the obedience of Christ

5c.   You have to diminish the _____ of this world that is coming into your _____, if you are going to take the limits off God.
Junk / heart

LESSON 2.1 • CARES OF THIS WORLD
DISCIPLESHIP QUESTIONS

1. According to Mark 4:18-19, what can happen when things of this world choke out the Word of God?
   A. You can't have children
   B. The Word becomes unfruitful
   C. You can lose your job
   D. All of the above
   E. None of the above

2. *Discussion question:* What are some things that choke the Word and limit what God can do in your life?

   _____
   _____
   _____

3. Psalm 46:10 says, *"Be _____, and _____ that I am God."*

4. If you are busy and have too much going on in the background of your life, what will happen?

   _____
   _____
   _____

5. What did Jesus say in Matthew 11:29?
   A. "I am the Son of God"
   B. "I am proud and arrogant in heart"
   C. "My yoke is easy and My burden is light"
   D. "I am mighty and awesome, and here is a fireworks display"
   E. "I am meek and lowly in heart"

6. *Discussion question:* Why do you think the main way you are going to relate to the Lord is through something subtle and simple?

   _____
   _____
   _____

DON'T LIMIT GOD

7. How often is God speaking to you?

_____

_____

_____

8. Why do many not like to be still?
   A. They begin to think of questions that make them uncomfortable
   B. They hear strange noises
   C. They get telephone calls and need to talk
   D. All of the above
   E. None of the above

9. *Discussion question:* Why do you think people tend to drown out uncomfortable questions and God's voice with busyness?

_____

_____

_____

10. What did Jesus have to do to recharge His spiritual batteries?
    A. Go on vacation
    B. Exercise His authority and demand His rest
    C. Stay up and commune with His Father
    D. All of the above
    E. None of the above

11. If Jesus needed to separate, do you need to follow His example and do the same?

_____

_____

_____

12. Your full potential is reached when you become _____ _____, not independent.

13. *Discussion question:* Why do you think God gave you a choice and told you to choose life (Deut. 30:19)?

_____

_____

_____

14. True or false: Worry is meditation in a negative form.

15. According to 2 Corinthians 10:4-5, what do you have the power to do?

    _____

    _____

    _____

16. You have to diminish the _____ of this world that is coming into your _____, if you are going to take the limits off God.

LESSON 2.1 • CARES OF THIS WORLD
ANSWER KEY

1. B. The Word becomes unfruitful
2. *Discussion question*
3. *Still / know*
4. You will limit your ability to hear God and will miss what He is telling you to do
5. E. "I am meek and lowly in heart"
6. *Discussion question*
7. Constantly
8. A. They begin to think of questions that make them uncomfortable
9. *Discussion question*
10. C. Stay up and commune with His Father
11. Yes
12. God dependent
13. *Discussion question*
14. True
15. Bring every thought into captivity to the obedience of Christ
16. Junk / heart

LESSON 2.1 • CARES OF THIS WORLD

SCRIPTURES

MARK 4:18-19

And these are they which are sown among thorns; such as hear the word, [**19**] And the cares of this world, and the deceitfulness of riches, and the lusts of other things entering in, choke the word, and it becometh unfruitful.

PSALM 46:10

Be still, and know that I am God: I will be exalted among the heathen, I will be exalted in the earth.

1 KINGS 19:11-12

And he said, Go forth, and stand upon the mount before the LORD. And, behold, the LORD passed by, and a great and strong wind rent the mountains, and brake in pieces the rocks before the LORD; but the LORD was not in the wind: and after the wind an earthquake; but the LORD was not in the earthquake: [**12**] And after the earthquake a fire; but the LORD was not in the fire: and after the fire a still small voice.

MATTHEW 11:29

Take my yoke upon you, and learn of me; for I am meek and lowly in heart: and ye shall find rest unto your souls.

PSALM 19:1

The heavens declare the glory of God; and the firmament sheweth his handywork.

MARK 6:31

And he said unto them, Come ye yourselves apart into a desert place, and rest a while: for there were many coming and going, and they had no leisure so much as to eat.

JEREMIAH 10:23

O LORD, I know that the way of man is not in himself: it is not in man that walketh to direct his steps.

DEUTERONOMY 30:19

I call heaven and earth to record this day against you, that I have set before you life and death, blessing and cursing: therefore choose life, that both thou and thy seed may live.

---

2 CORINTHIANS 10:4-5

(For the weapons of our warfare are not carnal, but mighty through God to the pulling down of strong holds;) [5] Casting down imaginations, and every high thing that exalteth itself against the knowledge of God, and bringing into captivity every thought to the obedience of Christ.

ISAIAH 26:3

Thou wilt keep him in perfect peace, whose mind is stayed on thee: because he trusteth in thee.

CARES OF THIS WORLD

And there was a certain disciple at Damascus, named Ananias; and to him said the Lord in a vision, Ananias. And he said, Behold, I am here, Lord.

ACTS 9:10

Most of you probably don't have this verse underlined in your Bible. But the Lord rang my bell through this scripture over forty years ago, and it changed my life. The Lord spoke to me through this verse and said, "Andrew, how many times have I called your name and you weren't there? You were doing something else." What would have happened if God had called Ananias and Ananias had been in such a state that the cares of this life, the deceitfulness of riches, and the lusts of other things were choking the Word, and he hadn't been able to listen to God? It's possible that God would've raised up someone else to minister to Saul. I'm not sure how it would have played out, but I'm sure we wouldn't be talking about Ananias today. How many of you has God spoken to and tried to keep you from making a mistake and tried to change your life and tried to do things in your life, but you weren't there because you were too busy or you were watching *As the Stomach Turns*?

Our lifestyles in America are not conducive to knowing God. If we are going to take the limits off God, we are going to have to start spending time with Him. We're going to have to renew our minds. The Word of God is so important. It will focus our attention on the things of God. If we are going to take the limits off God and begin to experience His best in our lives, we are going to have to start unplugging from this world and putting our minds on God and giving Him an opportunity to speak to us in that still, small voice.

I consciously take time off and spend time thinking about the Lord. I spend time walking on the trail I made outside my house. I spend time just sitting outside—looking around and thinking. These things are important. Our lifestyles have become so busy. This limits what God can do in our lives. If we want to be an inspiration to other people, we have to be inspired ourselves. We have to let God speak to us. We can't give to somebody else something we don't have. And most of us don't have God actively speaking in our lives because we are too busy to listen to Him or give Him any time.

GOD HAS CHOSEN THE FOOLISH THINGS

You should want to know God more. There's no telling how much I've missed when God tried to speak to me but I was too busy to hear what He was saying. However, I've also heard a lot because I've been available. There are many of you who are so talented that you depend only upon that talent and that you don't feel the need for God as much. You believe you can get things done on your own because you're motivated and talented. But I feel sorry for you. It's a blessing not to have any great talent, because it makes you dependent upon God.

> *But God hath chosen the foolish things of the world to confound the wise; and God hath chosen the weak things of the world to confound the things which are mighty.*
>
> 1 CORINTHIANS 1:27

God has not chosen the mighty, the rich, or the powerful. He has chosen the weak things of the world—the things that are despised. It's not because God's against people with money, education, talent, or ability. It's just that when people have it all in the natural, they tend to think they can do everything themselves, so they don't depend on God. The people who make a difference are those who don't have a lot, because they are turning to God and seeking Him; therefore, He can speak to them. God still speaks to the mighty and the talented, but the vast majority of them don't listen, because they aren't as dependent on Him.

It's an asset to know that you need God, that *"the way of man is not in himself"* (Jer. 10:23). You should spend a few days or a weekend fasting and praying—and not be distracted by food or anything else—and focus your attention on God and ask Him, "Is this all You have for my life? What do You have for me? Am I really where I'm supposed to be? Am I on target or am I off course?" If you gave God the total freedom and became still to let Him speak to you, many of you would be transformed. But most people do not give God that kind of time and stillness or listen to His voice that much. You need to do this on a regular basis.

Proverbs 4:26 tells us to *"ponder the path of thy feet, and let all thy ways be established."* You need to think about the path you're on. You need to ponder it. You need to meditate on it and be still. If you do, your path will be established.

I spend a lot of time pondering and thinking about what God has done in my life. I spend a lot of time remembering where I have come from and what God has spoken to me over the years. God has done so much for me. I constantly ponder and think about how God changed my life and how much He loves me.

If you are going to remove the limits from God and see His will come to pass in your life, you have to commit yourself to seeking God with all of your heart. You need to be still and let Him speak to you. You need to get quiet before God and listen. You might be looking for something more profound than this, but until you start doing these things, there's no point in going on to the next step.

MY SHEEP HEAR MY VOICE

We need to be focused on the Lord. We need to spend time with Him. If we don't do that, we will limit what He can do in our lives. God will not force us to do things. He will draw us and woo us and speak to us in a still, small voice. But if we have too much noise around us all of the time, we won't hear His voice. Then we'll wonder why He isn't speaking to us.

In John 10:27, Jesus said, "*My sheep* hear *my voice*" (emphasis mine). He didn't say, "My sheep *can* hear My voice." God is speaking to us every minute of every day. Every time we have a choice to make, God is giving us directions. If we are not hearing His voice, it's because we are dull of hearing—not because He is not speaking to us. We are drowning out His voice with other things. We need to change our lifestyles and focus our attention on God in order to take the limits off Him. We don't need to know everything before we step out. We just need to know that God is speaking to us.

LESSON 2.2 • CARES OF THIS WORLD
OUTLINE

VI.   What would have happened if God had called Ananias and he hadn't been able to listen to God?

And there was a certain disciple at Damascus, named Ananias; and to him said the Lord in a vision, Ananias. And he said, Behold, I am here, Lord.

ACTS 9:10

A. It's possible that God would've raised up someone else to minister to Saul.
B. How many of you has God spoken to but you weren't there because you were too busy?
C. If you are going to take the limits off God, you are going to have to start spending time with Him.
D. The Word of God is so important—it will focus your attention on the things of God.
E. You have to start unplugging from this world and putting your mind on God and giving Him an opportunity to speak to you in that still, small voice.

VII. There are many of you who are so talented that you depend only upon that talent and that you don't feel much need for God.

A. It's a blessing not to have any great talent, because it makes you dependent upon God.

But God hath chosen the foolish things of the world to confound the wise; and God hath chosen the weak things of the world to confound the things which are mighty.

1 CORINTHIANS 1:27

B. The people who make a difference are those who don't have a lot, because they are turning to God and seeking Him; therefore, He can speak to them.
C. God still speaks to the mighty and the talented, but the vast majority of them don't listen, because they aren't as dependent on Him.

VIII. Proverbs 4:26 says—

Ponder the path of thy feet, and let all thy ways be established.

A. You need to meditate on the path you're on and be still.
B. If you do, your path will be established.

C. If you are going to remove the limits from God and see His will come to pass in your life, you have to commit yourself to seeking Him with all of your heart.

D. You might be looking for something more profound than this, but until you start doing these things, there's no point in going on to the next step.

IX. *"My sheep* hear *my voice"* (John 10:27, emphasis mine).

A. Jesus didn't say, "My sheep *can* hear My voice."

B. Every time we have a choice to make, God is giving us directions.

C. If we are not hearing His voice, it's because we are dull of hearing—not because He is not speaking to us.

    i. We are drowning out His voice with other things.

D. We don't need to know everything before we step out; we just need to know that God is speaking to us.

TEACHER'S GUIDE

6.   What would have happened if God had called Ananias and he hadn't been able to listen to God?

   And there was a certain disciple at Damascus, named Ananias; and to him said the Lord in a vision, Ananias. And he said, Behold, I am here, Lord.
ACTS 9:10

It's possible that God would've raised up someone else to minister to Saul. How many of us has God spoken to but we weren't there because we were too busy? If we are going to take the limits off God, we are going to have to start spending time with Him. The Word of God is so important—it will focus our attention on the things of God. We have to start unplugging from this world and putting our minds on God and giving Him an opportunity to speak to us in that still, small voice.

6a.   *Discussion question:* What opportunities do you feel you may have missed because you were too busy to hear God?
   Discussion question
6b.   Why is the Word of God so important?
   It will focus your attention on the things of God
6c.   True or false: You have to start unplugging from this world and putting your mind on God and giving Him an opportunity to speak to you in that still, small voice.
   True

7. There are many of us who are so talented that we depend only upon that talent and that we don't feel much need for God. It's a blessing not to have any great talent, because it makes us dependent upon God.

> *But God hath chosen the foolish things of the world to confound the wise; and God hath chosen the weak things of the world to confound the things which are mighty.*
>
> 1 CORINTHIANS 1:27

The people who make a difference are those who don't have a lot, because they are turning to God and seeking Him; therefore, He can speak to them. God still speaks to the mighty and the talented, but the vast majority of them don't listen, because they aren't as dependent on Him.

7a. It's a _____ not to have any great talent, because it makes you
_____ on God.
Blessing / dependent

7b. Why don't the mighty and talented hear God speaking?
A. He isn't speaking to them
B. They don't listen
C. They aren't dependent on Him
D. A and C
E. B and C
E. B and C

8. Proverbs 4:26 says—

> *Ponder the path of thy feet, and let all thy ways be established.*

We need to meditate on the path we're on and be still. If we do, our path will be established. If we are going to remove the limits from God and see His will come to pass in our lives, we have to commit ourselves to seeking Him with all of our hearts. We might be looking for something more profound than this, but until we start doing these things, there's no point in going on to the next step.

8a. *Discussion question:* What do you think it means to *"ponder the path of thy feet"* (Prov. 4:26)?
Discussion question

8b. What will happen if you meditate on the path you're on and be still?
A. Your path will disappear
B. Your path will be established
C. Birds and deer will come to you
D. All of the above
E. None of the above
B. Your path will be established

9.   *"My sheep* hear *my voice"* (John 10:27, emphasis added). Jesus didn't say, "My sheep *can* hear My voice." Every time we have a choice to make, God is giving us directions. If we are not hearing His voice, it's because we are dull of hearing—not because He is not speaking to us. We are drowning out His voice with other things. We don't need to know everything before we step out; we just need to know that God is speaking to us.

9a.   *Discussion question:* What does John 10:27 mean to you?
       Discussion question

9b.   True or false: God isn't always giving directions.
       False

9c.   You don't need to know everything before you step out; you just need to know what?
       That God is speaking to you

LESSON 2.2 • CARES OF THIS WORLD
DISCIPLESHIP QUESTIONS

17. *Discussion question:* What opportunities do you feel you may have missed because you were too busy to hear God?

_____

_____

_____

18. Why is the Word of God so important?

_____

_____

_____

19. True or false: You have to start unplugging from this world and putting your mind on God and giving Him an opportunity to speak to you in that still, small voice.

20. It's a _____ not to have any great talent, because it makes you _____ on God.

21. Why don't the mighty and talented hear God speaking?
    A. He isn't speaking to them
    B. They don't listen
    C. They aren't dependent on Him
    D. A and C
    E. B and C

22. *Discussion question:* What do you think it means to *"ponder the path of thy feet"* (Prov. 4:26)?

_____

_____

_____

23. What will happen if you meditate on the path you're on and be still?
     A. Your path will disappear
     B. Your path will be established
     C. Birds and deer will come to you
     D. All of the above
     E. None of the above

24. *Discussion question:* What does John 10:27 mean to you?

     _____

     _____

     _____

25. True or false: God isn't always giving directions.

26. You don't need to know everything before you step out; you just need to know what?

     _____

     _____

     _____

LESSON 2.2 • CARES OF THIS WORLD
ANSWER KEY

17. *Discussion question*
18. It will focus your attention on the things of God
19. True
20. Blessing / dependent
21. E. B and C
22. *Discussion question*
23. B. Your path will be established
24. *Discussion question*
25. False
26. That God is speaking to you

LESSON 2.2 • CARES OF THIS WORLD
SCRIPTURES

ACTS 9:10

And there was a certain disciple at Damascus, named Ananias; and to him said the Lord in a vision, Ananias. And he said, Behold, I am here, Lord.

1 CORINTHIANS 1:27

But God hath chosen the foolish things of the world to confound the wise; and God hath chosen the weak things of the world to confound the things which are mighty.

JEREMIAH 10:23

O Lord, I know that the way of man is not in himself: it is not in man that walketh to direct his steps.

PROVERBS 4:26

Ponder the path of thy feet, and let all thy ways be established.

JOHN 10:27

My sheep hear my voice, and I know them, and they follow me.

FEAR OF RISK

Many people fear the unknown because there is risk involved. We fear being uncomfortable. We don't like being stretched. But if we aren't living on the edge, we are taking up too much space, and there's no way we'll avoid limiting God. It's exciting to be out there on the limb. My wife saw her mother and father get up every morning, go to work, come home, watch television, go to bed, and then do it all over again the next day. She prayed that her life would never be boring. Well, she got her prayer answered. Our lives are anything but boring!

Don't be content with doing nothing but surviving and getting by. There is more to life than that. You need to have a purpose. You need to have something that drives you. You need to believe God for something big. Some of you might think, *But if I was to do something risky, I might die.* But what's the difference between dying and having a slow death due to being miserable and depressed? You just need to throw caution to the wind and go for it!

We instinctively fear things we don't know. The Bible says—

There is no fear in love; but perfect love casteth out fear.

1 JOHN 4:18

If you really have a dynamic relationship with God, you don't need to fear the unknown. After all, you may not know what the future holds, but you know the One who holds the future. God is never going to do anything to hurt you. He's always going to do things to bless you.

You don't need to fear starting over again. Some people think, *If I go to Bible college, God might call me to go to Africa.* They are afraid of what God might ask them to do. But if God called them to Africa, they would love it! It'd be awesome!

Some people are just afraid to do anything. That's why they are failing. They are playing it too safe. Second Kings, chapter 7, is a good example of this:

And there were four leprous men at the entering in of the gate: and they said one to another, Why sit we here until we die? [4] If we say, We will enter into the city, then the famine is in the city, and we shall die there: and if we sit still here, we die also. Now therefore come, and let us fall unto the host of the Syrians: if they save us alive, we shall live; and if they kill us, we shall but die. [5] And they rose up in the twilight, to go unto the camp of the Syrians: and when they were come to the uttermost part of the camp of Syria, behold, there was no man there. [6] For the Lord had made the host of the Syrians to hear a noise of chariots, and a noise of horses, even the noise of a great host: and they said one to another, Lo, the king of Israel hath hired against us the kings of the Hittites, and the kings of the Egyptians, to come upon us. [7] Wherefore they arose and fled in the twilight, and left their tents, and their horses, and their asses, even the camp as it was, and fled for their life. [8] And when these lepers came to the uttermost part of the camp, they went into one tent, and did eat and drink, and carried thence silver, and gold, and raiment, and went and hid it; and came again, and entered into another tent, and carried thence also, and went and hid it. [9] Then they said one to another, We do not well: this day is a day of good tidings, and we hold our peace: if we tarry till the morning light, some mischief will come upon us: now therefore come, that we may go and tell the king's household.

2 KINGS 7:3-9

The Syrians had the people of God surrounded, and the siege had become so bad that they were actually selling animal dung at expensive prices. Two women killed one of their babies and ate him. The next day, they were going to kill the other baby and eat him also. This was a severe famine. And the scripture says that the four lepers said to each other, *"Why sit we here until we die?"* This has to be one of the most powerful statements in the Bible. Inside the city, people were eating their own children and animal dung! Can you imagine how bad it must have been outside the city for those outcasts?

If anybody should have been afraid to do something, it should have been these lepers. If they went into the city, they would die, but if they stayed outside the city, they would also die. They decided to go to the enemy, knowing that the worst thing that could happen to them was that they would die. I love that reasoning!

These four lepers were in dire straits, yet they said, *"Why sit we here until we die?"*

If we looked at this from an unemotional, logical standpoint, we would see that this was the smartest thing for the lepers to do. It was their only chance of survival. These lepers had to go out and take a risk. This was the only choice that made sense.

When the lepers got out there, the Lord caused the Syrians to hear the sound of an army. They thought the Israelites had hired the Egyptians to fight against them, so they panicked and fled. Food was still cooking on the fires, and they left their gold, silver, raiment, animals—everything!

When the lepers got to the Syrian camp, nobody was there, so they went in and found food and began to eat. They also found gold and silver. Instantly they went from a state of poverty and starvation to being the richest people around. They had so much they couldn't handle it all. Finally they said, "What we're doing isn't good. We need to go back and tell the people in Samaria what has happened." So, they went back and became heroes. And it was all because they took a chance by going out and facing the possibility of losing their lives. They took a risk!

When I was in the Baptist church, we used to sing a song that says, "Wherever He leads, we'll go." Then the missionaries would come up and talk about making a total commitment to the Lord, which usually meant going to Africa to live in a grass hut. They thought that if someone absolutely surrendered to God, He was going to do something terrible to them. But that is not the way God does things. He will send somebody to Africa, but when He does, He will put the desire in his or her heart to be there—that person will love it!

A SMASHING SUCCESS

Fear of failure is a big deal. When we are afraid of failure, we will not step out or risk doing what God told us to do. God has good plans for us (Jer. 29:11). We limit God when we are afraid to step out and do something because we think we might fail. I believe the biggest failure is when we play it too safe because we are afraid of making a mistake. We will all make mistakes. It will happen. But God is not going to fall off His throne because of it.

When we moved into the building that we are in right now, we moved from a 14,600-square-foot building to a 110,000-square-foot building. This was a major deal for us. And we did it debt free. It was awesome! When we were constructing our current facility, we tried to complete it by August so we could start the school year in the new building. But it wasn't finished until November.

During the dedication service, one of my students asked me if I was disappointed that we weren't able to move into our new building in August. I said, "No, I am not disappointed. I am just thrilled that we are here at all. We raised $3.2 million above our normal expenses in fourteen months. I'd call that a smashing success!"

We were shooting for August, but being three months late was no big deal. I've never done anything perfectly in my life, so it didn't bother me. If we shoot for the stars and miss but hit the moon, that's still better than what most people do.

If you're afraid of doing something because you may not do it perfectly, you'll never get anything done. You need to go for it! God's bigger than your mistakes.

FEAR OF FAILURE

Before God told me that I had limited Him, we had come to a place in our ministry where we were reaching people, finances were coming in, and it was relatively comfortable; so I didn't want to rock the boat. I didn't want to run the risk of failing. Fear of failure will make you fail worse than anything else. It's better to actually step out and believe God, and if you fail let God pick you up and dust you off so you can get up and go again. The worst failure of all is being paralyzed to the point that you do nothing.

You may be living very well. You may have trophies and awards sitting on your shelf, but you've never discovered the purpose you were created to fulfill. Maybe you've succeeded by your own strength and power. There are lost people who do that, but they aren't fulfilled in their hearts. They don't experience the same joy as those who know they're doing what God called them to do. You were made with a purpose. God's got more for you than what the vast majority of you are experiencing. You have to get rid of this fear of failure.

It's insanity to pray for your life to be different and then keep doing the same thing. If you do the same thing, you're going to get the same results. Do something different. Even if it's wrong, do something different. It would be better to run the risk of trying something else than to try nothing because you are afraid. Do something different! If nothing else, you'll find out that's not it and you can check one more thing off your list. Don't be afraid. The biggest failures in life are those who play it so conservatively that they don't risk anything.

You have to go for it! The world is looking for God. They are looking in all the wrong places, and one of the reasons is because the people who are born again aren't living in the fullness of their God-given calls. Your life should be a testimony. If you would catch on fire for God, the world would come and watch you burn!

How do we get rid of fear? Perfect love casts out fear (1 John 4:18). We need to recognize that God made us for a purpose. He designed us for a purpose. We have such a fear of being different that we don't want to get outside of the box. It's better to confront fear now than wait until we die and have the Lord ask, "Why didn't you do what I told you?"

We may reply, "Well, God, I made a lot of money. I was super successful. I was the head of the PTA. I was on the city council. I did this. I did that."

He will say, "But that's not what I called you to do. Why didn't you do what I called you to do?" All of our trophies and achievements aren't going to seem like very much if God says, "I created you for this, and you never did it. You never believed Me."

We may not have resisted it, but because of fear of failure, laziness, fear of change, or other reasons, we never really embraced it. If we stand before the Lord and He says, "Here is what I created you to do," we will say, "I knew that in my heart. That's a dream that I had. I knew that there was something more."

When we finally came to a place in our ministry where we weren't worried about how we were going to survive, we could've stayed at that place and God would've still loved me. But when I stand before the Lord someday, He would've said, "I called you to do a lot more than what you did, but you limited Me."

When God spoke to me about taking the limits off Him, we started expanding and getting aggressive. We were living on the edge. If God didn't come through—if this wasn't God—we were in big trouble. I became fearful. We had left that 14,000-square-foot building and moved into a 110,000-square-foot building. That was a little scary!

Looking back, we can see that the building has more than paid for itself. Our income has increased proportionally, so we have four to five times as much extra money as we had when we were doing things on a smaller scale. This is because we were where God told us to be. The blessings are so much greater now. What we are doing is much more beneficial. It'll be the same for you. God wants to prosper you. God wants to do something special in your life.

GOD'S WILL IS THE SAFEST PLACE ON EARTH

One of the reasons people struggle in their marriages and in other areas is because they aren't flowing with the plan God has for them. They become disappointed and discouraged. There is no place like being in the center of God's will.

Two days after the 9/11 attacks, one of my partners called me. His daughter was in the medical field, and she was heading to Afghanistan on a medical mission. He had his daughter on the extension phone and told me to tell her to cancel her trip. I asked her if she felt that God wanted her to go to Afghanistan.

She replied, "I know beyond any shadow of a doubt that this is what God has told me to do."

I said to her dad, "You know what? She needs to go."
He said, "How can you say that? She's putting herself in danger."

I told him, "Being in the center of God's will is the safest place on the face of the earth."

She ended up leaving for Afghanistan later that day. Everything turned out fine, and God blessed her.

In contrast, one of our very first Bible college students had a husband who wouldn't let her go on our missions trip because he was afraid of her flying. She stayed home against her wishes in order to submit to her husband. While we were on this missions trip, she was driving home and a teenager fell asleep at the wheel, crossed the median, and hit her. She ended up dying in this car wreck. She would've been much safer doing what God called her to do!

Any reasons you may have for not doing the will of God are not good enough. They are wrong. Being in the center of God's will is the safest, happiest, and most beneficial place to be. Just imagine that God Almighty, who has a universe to run and millions and millions of people talking to Him and asking Him for things, takes time to speak to you and place something in your heart. And for you to debate whether or not you will do what He says is beyond my comprehension. If I know that God wants me to do something, I'm going to do it or die trying. I am not going to live anywhere else but where I believe God wants me to be. And you should do the same.

If you feel that God has put something in your heart, do it! Maybe you aren't ready to do everything He's told you right now, but at least start moving in that direction. If you aren't completely sure of what God told you to do, put some motion to your boat, even if it's not full steam ahead. If you are sitting still, you can flip a rudder 360 degrees and it won't give any direction. You have to move. You have to do something. Say, "God, I am not absolutely sure, but I think this is it. I am going to move in this direction, and until I am sure, I'm going to test the waters and see what happens."

If you feel that God has spoken something to you, you know that you need to find His will for your life, or maybe you know His will for you, and for whatever reason you haven't been doing it, you are letting fear paralyze you. You need to repent and do what God has put in your heart. You must be determined not to rest until you find out what God wants you to do.

You must find and actively pursue God's purpose in order to have the real joy and peace of the Lord. There is a holy dissatisfaction that God places on the inside of you when you're off-track—when you know there's something more. I remember being in a service where I responded to an invitation similar to this. I spent all night walking in the bayous of Louisiana, praying, "God, I will find Your will for my life. I will do what You called me to do." God honored that prayer, and it changed my life. He will do the same for you!

ANDREW'S RECOMMENDATIONS FOR FURTHER STUDY

When you start moving, God will give you direction. Commit yourself to doing something. If nothing else, commit yourself to discovering God's will for your life. I have a teaching entitled *How to Find, Follow, and Fulfill God's Will.* This will be a great tool to help you find God's will for your life. You aren't going to fulfill His will accidentally; you have to do it on purpose.

LESSON 3.1 • FEAR OF RISK
OUTLINE

I.   Many people fear the unknown because there is risk involved.
   A. If you really have a dynamic relationship with God, you don't need to fear the unknown (1 John 4:18).
   B. God is never going to do anything to hurt you.
   C. He's always going to do things to bless you.
   D. You don't need to fear starting over again.

II. Some people are just afraid to do anything.
   A. That's why they're failing—they are playing it too safe.
   B. Second Kings 7:3-9 is a good example of this.
     i. The Scripture says that the four lepers said to each other, *"Why sit we here until we die?"*
     ii. They decided to take a risk and go to the enemy, knowing that the worst thing that could happen to them is that they would die.
     iii. If we looked at this choice from an unemotional, logical standpoint, we would see that this was the smartest thing for the lepers to do.
     iv. When the lepers got out there, the Lord caused the Syrians to hear the sound of an army, so the Syrians panicked and fled, leaving behind all their possessions.
     v. Instantly the lepers went from a state of poverty and starvation to being the richest people around.
     vi. It was all because they took a chance by going out and facing the possibility of losing their lives.

III. Fear of failure is a big deal.
   A. We limit God when we are afraid to step out and do something because we think we might fail.
   B. I believe that the biggest failure is when we play it too safe because we are afraid of making a mistake, but we will all make mistakes.
   C. If we're afraid of doing something because we may not do it perfectly, we'll never get anything done.
   D. It's better to actually step out and believe God and, if we fail, let God pick us up and dust us off so we can get up and go again.

IV. The world is looking for God.
    A. They are looking in all the wrong places, and one of the reasons is because the people who are born again aren't living in the fullness of their God-given calls.
    B. Your life should be a testimony.
    C. If you would catch on fire for God, the world would come and watch you burn!

V. We need to recognize that God made us for a purpose.
    A. All of our trophies and achievements aren't going to seem like very much if God says, "I created you for this, and you never did it. You never believed Me."
    B. We may not have resisted God's purpose for us, but because of a fear of failure, laziness, fear of change, or other reasons, we may not have really embraced it.
    C. But God wants to do something special in our lives.

VI. There is no place like being in the center of God's will.
    A. Any reasons you may have for not doing the will of God are not good enough—they are wrong.
    B. Being in the center of God's will is the safest, happiest, and most beneficial place to be.
    C. I am not going to live anywhere else but where I believe God wants me to be, and you should do the same.

VII. If you feel that God has put something in your heart, do it!
    A. Maybe you aren't ready to do everything He's told you right now, but at least start moving in that direction.
    B. If you aren't completely sure of what God told you to do, put some motion to your boat, even if it's not full steam ahead.
    C. You must find and actively pursue God's purpose in order to have the real joy and peace of the Lord.
    D. There is a holy dissatisfaction that God places on the inside of you when you're off-track—when you know there's something more.

ANDREW'S RECOMMENDATIONS FOR FURTHER STUDY

When you start moving, God will give you direction. Commit yourself to doing something. If nothing else, commit yourself to discovering God's will for your life. I have a teaching entitled *How to Find, Follow, and Fulfill God's Will*. This will be a great tool to help you find God's will for your life. You aren't going to fulfill His will accidentally; you have to do it on purpose.

LESSON 3.1 • FEAR OF RISK
TEACHER'S GUIDE

1.   Many people fear the unknown because there is risk involved. If we really have a dynamic relationship with God, we don't need to fear the unknown (1 John 4:18). God is never going to do anything to hurt us. He's always going to do things to bless us. We don't need to fear starting over again.

1a.   True or false: Many people fear the unknown because there is risk involved.
True

1b.   Why do you not need to fear starting over again?
Because God is never going to do anything to hurt you and is always going to do things to bless you

2.   Some people are just afraid to do anything. That's why they're failing—they are playing it too safe. Second Kings 7:3-9 is a good example of this. The Scripture says that the four lepers said to each other, *"Why sit we here until we die?"* They decided to take a risk and go to the enemy, knowing that the worst thing that could happen to them is that they would die. If we looked at this choice from an unemotional, logical standpoint, we would see that this was the smartest thing for the lepers to do. When the lepers got out there, the Lord caused the Syrians to hear the sound of an army, so the Syrians panicked and fled, leaving behind all their possessions. Instantly the lepers went from a state of poverty and starvation to being the richest people around. It was all because they took a chance by going out and facing the possibility of losing their lives.

2a.   Why are some people failing?
    A. They aren't trying hard enough
    B. They didn't say the right prayer
    C. They are playing it too safe
    D. All of the above
    E. None of the above
    C. They are playing it too safe

2b.   *Discussion question:* What lessons can you take from the story of the lepers and apply to your life?
Discussion question

3.	Fear of failure is a big deal. We limit God when we are afraid to step out and do something because we think we might fail. I believe that the biggest failure is when we play it too safe because we are afraid of making a mistake, but we will all make mistakes. If we're afraid of doing something because we may not do it perfectly, we'll never get anything done. It's better to actually step out and believe God and, if we fail, let God pick us up and dust us off so we can get up and go again.

3a.	True or false: If you know you will make a mistake, it's better to play it safe.
	False

3b.	*Discussion question:* Why do you think Andrew says that is it better to step out and believe God and, if you fail, let God pick you up and dust you off so you can get up and go again?
	Discussion question

4.	The world is looking for God. They are looking in all the wrong places, and one of the reasons is because the people who are born again aren't living in the fullness of their God-given calls. Our lives should be a testimony. If we would catch on fire for God, the world would come and watch us burn!

4a.	Why do people in the world either not find God or look for Him in the wrong places?
	People who are born again aren't living in the fullness of their God-given calls

4b.	Your life should be a _____.
	Testimony

5.	We need to recognize that God made us for a purpose. All of our trophies and achievements aren't going to seem like very much if God says, "I created you for this, and you never did it. You never believed Me." We may not have resisted God's purpose for us, but because of a fear of failure, laziness, fear of change, or other reasons, we may not have really embraced it. But God wants to do something special in our lives.

5a.	*Discussion question:* What do you think has kept you from embracing God's purpose for you?
	Discussion question

6.   There is no place like being in the center of God's will. Any reasons we may have for not doing the will of God are not good enough—they are wrong. Being in the center of God's will is the safest, happiest, and most beneficial place to be. Andrew is not going to live anywhere else but where he believes God wants him to be, and we should do the same.

6a.   Any reason you may have for not doing God's will is what?
      Not good enough and/or wrong

6b.   Being in the center of God's will is the _____, _____, and most _____ place to be.
      Safest / happiest / beneficial

6c.   *Discussion question:* Why should you not live anywhere else but where you believe God wants you to be?
      Discussion question

7.   If we feel that God has put something in our hearts, let's do it! Maybe we aren't ready to do everything He's told us right now, but we should at least start moving in that direction. If we aren't completely sure of what God told us to do, we need to put some motion to our boats, even if it's not full steam ahead. We must find and actively pursue God's purpose in order to have the real joy and peace of the Lord. There is a holy dissatisfaction that God places on the inside of us when we're off-track—when we know there's something more.

7a.   True or false: If you believe God has put something in your heart, the best thing is to do it.
      True

7b.   If you aren't ready to do everything He's told you right now, at least start _____ in that direction.
      Moving

7c.   When does a holy dissatisfaction come on you?
      A.   When you see man's unrighteousness
      B.   When you're off-track from God's purpose
      C.   When you can't find the right Bible
      D.   All of the above
      E.   None of the above
      B. When you're off-track from God's purpose

LESSON 3.1 • FEAR OF RISK
DISCIPLESHIP QUESTIONS

1.   True or false: Many people fear the unknown because there is risk involved.

2.   Why do you not need to fear starting over again?

   _____

   _____

   _____

3.   Why are some people failing?
   A.   They aren't trying hard enough
   B.   They didn't say the right prayer
   C.   They are playing it too safe
   D.   All of the above
   E.   None of the above

4.   *Discussion question:* What lessons can you take from the story of the lepers and apply to your life?

   _____

   _____

   _____

5.   True or false: If you know you will make a mistake, it's better to play it safe.

6.   *Discussion question:* Why do you think Andrew says that is it better to step out and believe God and, if you fail, let God pick you up and dust you off so you can get up and go again?

   _____

   _____

   _____

7.   Why do people in the world either not find God or look for Him in the wrong places?

   _____

   _____

   _____

8.   Your life should be a _____.

DON'T LIMIT GOD

9. *Discussion question:* What do you think has kept you from embracing God's purpose for you?

    _____

    _____

    _____

10. Any reason you may have for not doing God's will is what?

    _____

    _____

    _____

11. Being in the center of God's will is the _____, _____, and most _____ place to be.

12. *Discussion question:* Why should you not live anywhere else but where you believe God wants you to be?

    _____

    _____

    _____

13. True or false: If you believe God has put something in your heart, the best thing is to do it.

14. If you aren't ready to do everything He's told you right now, at least start _____ in that direction.

15. When does a holy dissatisfaction come on you?
    A. When you see man's unrighteousness
    B. When you're off-track from God's purpose
    C. When you can't find the right Bible
    D. All of the above
    E. None of the above

LESSON 3.1 • FEAR OF RISK
ANSWER KEY

1. True
2. Because God is never going to do anything to hurt you and is always going to do things to bless you
3. C. They are playing it too safe
4. *Discussion question*
5. False
6. *Discussion question*
7. People who are born again aren't living in the fullness of their God-given calls
8. Testimony
9. *Discussion question*
10. Not good enough and/or wrong
11. Safest / happiest / beneficial
12. *Discussion question*
13. True
14. Moving
15. B. When you're off-track from God's purpose

LESSON 3.1 • FEAR OF RISK
SCRIPTURES

1 JOHN 4:18

There is no fear in love; but perfect love casteth out fear: because fear hath torment. He that feareth is not made perfect in love.

2 KINGS 7:3-9

And there were four leprous men at the entering in of the gate: and they said one to another, Why sit we here until we die? [4] If we say, We will enter into the city, then the famine is in the city, and we shall die there: and if we sit still here, we die also. Now therefore come, and let us fall unto the host of the Syrians: if they save us alive, we shall live; and if they kill us, we shall but die. [5] And they rose up in the twilight, to go unto the camp of the Syrians: and when they were come to the uttermost part of the camp of Syria, behold, there was no man there. [6] For the Lord had made the host of the Syrians to hear a noise of chariots, and a noise of horses, even the noise of a great host: and they said one to another, Lo, the king of Israel hath hired against us the kings of the Hittites, and the kings of the Egyptians, to come upon us. [7] Wherefore they arose and fled in the twilight, and left their tents, and their horses, and their asses, even the camp as it was, and fled for their life. [8] And when these lepers came to the uttermost part of the camp, they went into one tent, and did eat and drink, and carried thence silver, and gold, and raiment, and went and hid it; and came again, and entered into another tent, and carried thence also, and went and hid it. [9] Then they said one to another, We do not well: this day is a day of good tidings, and we hold our peace: if we tarry till the morning light, some mischief will come upon us: now therefore come, that we may go and tell the king's household.

JEREMIAH 29:11

For I know the thoughts that I think toward you, saith the Lord, thoughts of peace, and not of evil, to give you an expected end.

FEAR OF RISK

One time a friend contacted me and said he was starting a Bible school. He had four pages of good questions he wanted to ask me about starting this school. One of the questions was, "If you were doing it all over again, what would you do differently?" I thought about it, and you know what? I wouldn't have done anything differently.

Our Bible school has changed a lot since it first started. It's much better than it was, but at the time, I gave it everything I had. I didn't have very many resources, so I couldn't do things the way that we do them now. I also didn't have the same personnel. There were so many limitations in the beginning.

If I had said "I'm going to do this Bible college perfectly, and it's going to be the best Bible college that ever existed," we never would have started a Bible college. We had to start with what we had, and yes, we made some mistakes. Yes, we've learned some things. That's why it's much better today than it was when we first started.

Some people are such perfectionists that they are afraid of making a mistake, so they don't do anything. That's the biggest mistake of all. It's like a little kid learning to ride a bicycle. He will fall. He may cut his knee. But you know what? He will get back up and do it again. Eventually, he will learn how to ride a bicycle.

People fear making mistakes. This really comes down to the fact that they aren't secure in Jesus. They are afraid because their identity and worth are caught up in what they do. But that's not the way it should be. We need to find our security and identity in our relationship with God. If my ministry failed and I had to go back to pouring concrete for a living, I know that God would still love me. I could have a wonderful relationship with Him without a ministry. My identity is not in my ministry. That is not who I am. That is just a vehicle that God has given me to use while I'm on the earth.

My board of directors once told me, "Andrew, you're bankrupt. Close the doors. We're shutting this thing down!" They were going to shut our ministry down because we couldn't make it financially. When I thought about this, I actually got excited. I thought, *This will be awesome! My relationship with God will go through the roof if I don't have all of the things of the ministry to deal with. It would be great to be "Joe Blow Christian," just in love with Jesus, and have no ministerial responsibility.* I knew that wasn't what the Lord wanted me to do, but I would have been content to walk away from this ministry. We need to find our identity in the Lord and be secure in Him.

STEP OUT OF THE BOAT

Over the years, as I believed God for various things to come to pass, I realized that even if they didn't, God would still be pleased with me because at least I went for it. I believe He would have said, "Andrew, you failed, but I'm proud of you because you tried." Then He would've proceeded to show me where I missed it. I think that's the way God looks at things—and at us.

Many of you are limiting God because you aren't doing what God has put in your heart due to the risk involved. You're afraid to get out of the boat. You're afraid to do something out of the norm. Are you afraid to quit your job and move, leaving your family and friends, in order to go to Bible college—or do whatever else God has told you to do?

When I began in ministry, I used to go to nursing homes and prisons because they'd let anybody preach! That was really good for me. I remember one lady in particular, at the nursing home because she was so proper. You could tell she was very well-to-do when she was younger. She always looked picture perfect—every hair was in place, and she wore expensive clothing. When I came to see her, she spent the whole time crying and talking about how she used to be somebody important and how people used to come and seek her out. She still had friends, but sometimes it was months before someone came to see her. She was just sitting there waiting on death. I remember looking at her and thinking, *God, I don't want my life to be this way.*

Just about everyone is going to get old. When you get old, will you just sit around and wait on death? Is your life so wrapped up in your job that when you retire, your life will be over? I don't want that, and I don't think you want that either. But that's where a lot of people are headed because they are afraid to step out of the boat. They are afraid to follow what God told them to do. They are taking the easy way out.

I've actually had people tell me that God told them to come to our Bible school. But they still had five years before they could retire, so they couldn't leave at that time without losing some of their pension. I told them that God can give them a lot more than their pension. When God called them to go, He knew they still had five years left before they could retire with a pension. Yet He still called them!

They limit God because of fear. They are counting on their Social Security check instead of God. If you can't believe God for something more than Social Security, I'm not sure He needs you. I opted out of Social Security when I was twenty years old, and I don't have a penny coming. But guess what? God has taken care of me. Everything Jamie and I own is paid for. We do not have to limit ourselves to a pension plan. God is bigger than that! You need to step out of the boat and trust God. It's exciting to be out there, saying, "God, if You don't come through, I'm going to make a huge splash!"

IT'S EXCITING TO SERVE GOD

I've actually reached a place in my life that when everything is going well and I don't have any challenges—or when God isn't asking me to do something that's bigger than myself—it's boring. I'm a pretty bland person, so people think I don't ever do anything exciting or fun, but everyone has some outlet. My outlet is four-wheeling over mountain passes with a thousand-foot drop straight down. I just think that's awesome!

Once, I drove my pickup across a gorge known as the Devil's Punchbowl. It was 100 or 200 feet deep. You have to make a right-hand turn, and there are only two steel beams across the gorge—no planks or anything. It was exciting! Jamie was screaming a little and has refused to ever let me go over this gorge again. But to me, this was fun!

If your life doesn't have a little bit of excitement in it, you might as well say, "God, I'll go anywhere or do anything You want." Follow through on it, and I guarantee God will make your life exciting. You might think, *But I might fail.* Yes, you might. Proverbs 24:16 says that a righteous man will get up seven times. You don't have to be afraid of taking a risk and failing. Take the limits off God, step out in faith, and do what He has called you to do!

> *For the eyes of the LORD run to and fro throughout the whole earth, to shew himself strong in the behalf of them whose heart is perfect toward him.*
>
> 2 CHRONICLES 16:9

Being perfect doesn't mean you are sinless. Here, God was referring to people who are committed to Him and telling Him, "God, I'll do anything. I'll say whatever You want me to say. I'll go wherever You want me to go. Just tell me what to do, and I'll follow You to the best of my ability." God is looking throughout the whole earth for people like this. Are you willing to risk it all to follow Him? Your response should be, "God, look no further. Here I am."

TOTALLY COMMITTED

Dwight L. Moody once attended a service in Chicago where he heard a preacher make the following statement: "The world has never seen what God can do through one person who is totally committed to Him." Dwight stood up and said, "I'll be that man," even though he only had a third-grade education and could barely read. When Dwight preached, he would read a passage of Scripture up to a word that he didn't know, then stop and preach on it. Then he would start on the other side of that word, so people wouldn't know that he couldn't read.

Dwight L. Moody was rejected by three churches. He tried to join them, but they didn't consider him to be a good enough Christian to be a member of their churches. They rejected him from being a member, yet he preached to crowds of 150,000 before they even had microphones. He preached to kings and impacted every continent on the face of the earth. He was the Billy Graham of his day. He saw miracle after miracle, and amazing things happened through his ministry.

You may have some things in your heart that would cause you to live your life differently if you didn't have restrictions. Yet fear is causing you to limit yourself and limit what God can do, because you're afraid that you might not prosper as much as you are prospering now. You are afraid that people might criticize you or that something negative might happen.

Before I die, I believe I will accomplish everything that God has put on the inside of me. I can truthfully say that right now I am in the process of doing everything that God has placed in my heart, and I know that as I continue to grow, He will give me more things to do. I haven't arrived, but I've left. I am moving in the right direction.

YOU HAVE POTENTIAL

One Christian motivational speaker has been known to say that if you want to go to a place that has the most potential, go to a graveyard. The vast majority of people take their potential to the grave, dying without ever realizing their full potential. Hundreds of people have dreams and goals that have been set aside. They have let life limit them; therefore, they limit God.

Sometimes when I teach, I ask, "Are you reaching your potential? Are you doing what God really put in your heart?" Then when I give an invitation, 80 to 90 percent of the crowd will stand and admit they don't know for sure that they are doing what God called them to do.

How can people live like that? It has been about forty-five years since I have done my own thing. During this time, I've been following the leadership of God to the best of my ability. I haven't done it perfectly, but I've been seeking to follow God. And it has been awesome!

I can't even relate to people who are living their lives and just letting circumstances dictate to them. They get a job because they have to make a living. They don't have a purpose. They don't know what God put them here for. They aren't doing what God has equipped them to do. They aren't reaching their full potential. That's not life. That's not living. That's just surviving.

God wants us to be practical: We need to take care of ourselves and our family. But in the process, we need to start dreaming and believing God for those dreams in our hearts to come to pass. We need to say, "Father, show me how I can make my life count."

When I die, I want people to miss me and say "Things were better because Andrew was around" instead of saying "Well, praise God, he's gone!" Our lives should be touching others and making a difference. Yet many of us are just living normal, substandard lives because we're afraid of taking risks.

FEAR OF CHANGE

Another fear that hinders people is the fear of change. Many of us are afraid to do something different. Resistance to change is really strong in our culture. We aren't as grounded in tradition as some other cultures are, but tradition is still strong in America. Just try pastoring a church, or ask a pastor. I guarantee they'll say it's nearly impossible to get people to change.

One of the reasons people resist change is because they're lazy. It takes effort to change. I have a book entitled *Effortless Change*. In this book, I talk about how we can change effortlessly, but there's even an "effort" in that. The effort is getting into the Word of God and renewing our minds. Then as we think, that's the way we'll become (Prov. 23:7).

Most of us just want to sit on our couches, watch something on television, and be mesmerized. When we say that someone is mesmerized by something, it means that person has given themselves over to and is being controlled by that thing. This is the way we are with television. We turn it on and sit there, forgetting about everything else. We come under the control of the television.

Did you know that you can become comfortable and get to a place where you stop stretching yourself? This can be seen in a lot of older people who have raised their families or have worked all their lives and are now ready to retire. They want to enjoy their grandkids, travel, and have a good time.

There's nothing wrong with people enjoying the fruits of their labor, but I guarantee you, the moment they retire and start doing nothing, their health will begin to decline.

God didn't make us to sit and coast through life. We will last longer, be happier and more productive, and everything will work better in our lives when we have a purpose. The most fruitful people who come into our Bible colleges are those who are retired. They come to learn the Word of God. They don't have the same pressures and demands that they had in the past. We have retired people from all over the world who put their lives on the line by going to third-world countries where they face sickness and disease in different cultures—and they are loving it!

DON'T QUIT!

Jamie and I have been in ministry for over forty-five years. We've been through a lot of hard times. Once, I was talking with a group of preachers about some of the tough times we'd gone through. I told them about the financial problems Jamie and I had faced, such as when we hadn't eaten in two weeks during the time that Jamie was eight months' pregnant. They said to me, "My God, what you did to Jamie is worse than anything we ever did to our wives." Yet these men had committed adultery, lied, stolen, and gone to jail. They had done all these terrible things, and they still thought what Jamie went through was a lot worse!

I've been through a lot of hardship in my life. I think Jamie is the only woman on the planet who would have stuck with me through what we have gone through. Radio broadcaster Paul Harvey even noted on his broadcast once that one particular hardship of ours was one of the worst things he had ever heard in his life.

The Lord spoke to me in a dream on July 26, 1999. He told me I was just now starting my ministry. This was after I had been in ministry for thirty-one years! If something had happened and I had died, I would have missed what God called me to do. This was both encouraging and discouraging at the same time. It was discouraging because I spent thirty-one years in ministry being schooled for the ministry God had called me to. On the other hand, it was encouraging because we had seen some great things happen over those thirty-one years. So, if I was just starting my ministry, that meant it was only going to get better!

When we started on television on January 3, 2000, we hit a place where things were working nearly effortlessly. Before that time, it was a struggle. We were on the verge of disaster. It looked like our ministry could die at any moment. Then, all of a sudden, things just began to work. There was an anointing that wasn't present before. People began responding to our message and our ministry.

Over the next two years, our ministry doubled. Finally, there was light at the end of the tunnel, and it wasn't a train! We were going to make it. We were going to survive. We actually started seeing people's lives change. The lesson is, though we'd had problems all the years prior to that, we didn't get lazy and quit. We would have limited what God wanted to do in our lives if we had.

We don't need to *rust* out; we need to *wear* out. We need to *burn* out serving God. We can rest throughout all of eternity. People are resistant to change because they've made their "nests." They limit God because they have it nice. They are lazy. They are comfortable. That's not a good place to be. I've just given up on ever getting to a place where I coast. Right now in our ministry, we are believing God for bigger things than ever before. I'm never going to quit dreaming! Until I go to be with the Lord, I am going to be working on something. I am so thankful I have a purpose that is going to keep me going until I draw my last breath. There will never be an end to what I'm doing. I believe that I'll leave this earth preaching!

SATISFACTION AND CONTENTMENT

God will call us to do something beyond ourselves. He called me to preach, and I was an introvert who couldn't even look at a person in the face while talking. Now I talk to millions of people. God asks us to do things that we can't do. This makes us dependent on Him. If we're just doing what we can do, we've missed God. God is calling us for something special, and some element of risk will be involved.

The perfect love of God will cast out fear. If you really knew the plans that God has for you and what He wants to do with your life, you would realize there's more than what you are doing. Your life would be more fulfilling and more satisfying. There are a satisfaction and a contentment that come when you know that you are doing what God called you to do. But you will never experience that satisfaction while doing your own thing or whatever opportunity presents.

You need to get rid of this fear of failure and recognize that if you aren't stretching yourself and seeking after God's will for your life with everything you've got, you are failing.

> *I beseech you therefore, brethren, by the mercies of God, that ye present your bodies a living sacrifice, holy, acceptable unto God, which is your reasonable service. [2] And be not conformed to this world: but be ye transformed by the renewing of your mind, that ye may prove what is that good, and acceptable, and perfect, will of God.*
>
> ROMANS 12:1-2

This isn't just for full-time preachers or ministers. This is for every Joe Blow and Jane Doe Christian—every one of us. It's our normal Christian duty. Jesus died for us, so we should live for Him.

We should commit ourselves without any questions. If the Lord asks us to do something, we need to say, "God, I'll go anywhere. I'll do anything. Whatever You want me to do, I'll do."

If you haven't reached that place yet, you are limiting God because you are afraid of what He's going to ask you to do or what it's going to cost. God is the biggest giver who ever existed. God will never let you out-give Him. When God sees you giving something up and putting yourself at risk to follow Him, He will always wind up blessing you more than you ever bless Him. Take the limits off God, and watch His blessings overtake you!

ANDREW'S RECOMMENDATIONS FOR FURTHER STUDY

I have a book entitled *Effortless Change.* In this book, I talk about how we can change effortlessly, but there's even an "effort" in that. The effort is getting into the Word of God and renewing our minds. Then as we think, that's the way we'll become (Prov. 23:7).

LESSON 3.2 • FEAR OF RISK
OUTLINE

VIII. People fear making mistakes.
   A. This really comes down to the fact that they aren't secure in Jesus.
   B. They are afraid because their identity and worth are caught up in what they do.
   C. We need to find our security and identity in our relationship with God.

IX. Many of you may be limiting God because you aren't doing what God has put in your heart due to the risk involved.
   A. You're afraid to get out of the boat.
   B. When you get old, will you just sit around and wait on death?
   C. That's where a lot of people are headed—they are afraid to follow what God has told them to do.
   D. But it's exciting to be out there saying, "God, if You don't come through, I'm going to make a huge splash!"

X. If your life doesn't have a little bit of excitement in it, you might as well say, "God, I'll go anywhere or do anything You want."
   A. Follow through on it, and I guarantee that God will make your life exciting.
   B. You might fail, but Proverbs 24:16 says that a righteous man will get up seven times.
   C. Being perfect doesn't mean you are sinless.

   For the eyes of the LORD run to and fro throughout the whole earth, to shew himself strong in the behalf of them whose heart is perfect toward him.
   2 CHRONICLES 16:9

   D. God was referring to people who are committed to Him.
   E. God is looking throughout the whole earth for people like this.
   F. Are you willing to risk it all to follow Him?

XI. You may have some things in your heart that would cause you to live your life differently if you didn't have restrictions.
   A. Fear is causing you to limit yourself and limit what God can do, because you're afraid that you might not prosper as much as you are prospering now.
   B. You are afraid that people might criticize you or that something negative might happen.

XII. The vast majority of people take their potential to the grave, dying without ever realizing their full potential.
   A. Hundreds of people have dreams and goals that have been set aside.
   B. They have let life limit them; therefore, they limit God.
   C. I can't even relate to people who are living their lives and just letting circumstances dictate to them.
   D. They don't know what God put them here for, they aren't doing what God has equipped them to do, and they aren't reaching their full potential.
   E. That's not living—that's just surviving.

XIII. God wants us to be practical.
   A. We need to take care of ourselves and our family.
   B. But in the process, we need to start dreaming and believing God for those dreams in our hearts to come to pass.
   C. We need to say, "Father, show me how I can make my life count."
   D. Our lives should be touching others and making a difference.

XIV. Another fear that hinders people is the fear of change.
   A. Resistance to change is really strong in our culture.
   B. One of the reasons people resist change is because they're lazy.
   C. It takes effort to change.
   D. God didn't make us to sit and coast through life.
   E. We will last longer, be happier and more productive, and everything will work better in our lives when we have a purpose.
   F. We don't need to *rust* out; we need to *wear* out.
   G. I am so thankful I have a purpose that is going to keep me going until I draw my last breath.

XV. God will call us to do something beyond ourselves.
   A. This makes us dependent on Him.
   B. If we're just doing what we can do, we've missed God.
   C. If we really knew the plans that God has for us and what He wants to do with our lives, we would realize there's more than what we are doing.
   D. There are a satisfaction and a contentment that come when we know that we are doing what God called us to do.

I beseech you therefore, brethren, by the mercies of God, that ye present your bodies a living sacrifice, holy, acceptable unto God, which is your reasonable service. [2] And be not conformed to this world: but be ye transformed by the renewing of your mind, that ye may prove what is that good, and acceptable, and perfect, will of God.

ROMANS 12:1-2

E. This isn't just for full-time preachers or ministers—it's our normal Christian duty.

F. Jesus died for us, so we should live for Him.

G. We should commit ourselves without any questions.

H. Let's take the limits off God, and we'll watch His blessings overtake us!

ANDREW'S RECOMMENDATIONS FOR FURTHER STUDY

I have a book entitled *Effortless Change.* In this book, I talk about how we can change effortlessly, but there's even an "effort" in that. The effort is getting into the Word of God and renewing our minds. Then as we think, that's the way we'll become (Prov. 23:7).

LESSON 3.2 • FEAR OF RISK
TEACHER'S GUIDE

8.   People fear making mistakes. This really comes down to the fact that they aren't secure in Jesus. They are afraid because their identity and worth are caught up in what they do. We need to find our security and identity in our relationship with God.

8a.   Why do people fear that they will make mistakes?
They aren't secure in Jesus

8b.   *Discussion question:* Why is it so important to find your security and identity in your relationship with God?
Discussion question

9.   Many of us may be limiting God because we aren't doing what God has put in our hearts due to the risk involved. We're afraid to get out of the boat. When we get old, will we just sit around and wait on death? That's where a lot of people are headed—they are afraid to follow what God has told them to do. But it's exciting to be out there saying, "God, if You don't come through, I'm going to make a huge splash!"

9a.   *Discussion question:* When you get old, will you just sit around and wait on death?
Discussion question

10. If our lives don't have a little bit of excitement in them, we might as well say, "God, I'll go anywhere or do anything You want." If we follow through on it, God will make our lives exciting. We might fail, but Proverbs 24:16 says that a righteous man will get up seven times. Being perfect doesn't mean we are sinless.

> *For the eyes of the LORD run to and fro throughout the whole earth, to shew himself strong in the behalf of them whose heart is perfect toward him.*
> 2 CHRONICLES 16:9

God was referring to people who are committed to Him. God is looking throughout the whole earth for people like this. Are we willing to risk it all to follow Him?

10a. By telling God, "I'll go anywhere or do anything You want," what will you bring into your life?
    A. Excitement
    B. Trouble
    C. Resistance
    D. All of the above
    E. None of the above
    A. Excitement
10b. True or false: Being perfect means you are sinless.
    False
10c. In 2 Chronicles 16:9, God was referring to people who are _____ to Him.
    Committed

11. We may have some things in our hearts that would cause us to live our lives differently if we didn't have restrictions. Fear is causing us to limit ourselves and limit what God can do, because we're afraid that we might not prosper as much as we are prospering now. We are afraid that people might criticize us or that something negative might happen.

11a. What are some fears that may be limiting you and limiting what God can do?
    A. You may not prosper as much as you are now
    B. People may criticize you
    C. Something negative might happen
    D. All of the above
    E. None of the above
    D. All of the above

12. The vast majority of people take their potential to the grave, dying without ever realizing their full potential. Hundreds of people have dreams and goals that have been set aside. They have let life limit them; therefore, they limit God. Andrew can't even relate to people who are living their lives and just letting circumstances dictate to them. They don't know what God put them here for, they aren't doing what God has equipped them to do, and they aren't reaching their full potential. That's not living—that's just surviving.

12a. For the vast majority of people, where does their potential end up?
   In the grave
12b. Why do most people die without realizing their full potential?
   They set aside their dreams and goals—they let life limit them
12c. If you don't know what God put you here for, aren't doing what God has equipped you to do, and aren't reaching your full potential, is that living?
   No, it's just surviving

13. God wants us to be practical. We need to take care of ourselves and our family. But in the process, we need to start dreaming and believing God for those dreams in our hearts to come to pass. We need to say, "Father, show me how I can make my life count." Our lives should be touching others and making a difference.

13a. *Discussion question:* In what ways should your life be touching others and making a difference?
   Discussion question

14. Another fear that hinders people is the fear of change. Resistance to change is really strong in our culture. One of the reasons people resist change is because they're lazy. It takes effort to change. God didn't make us to sit and coast through life. We will last longer, be happier and more productive, and everything will work better in our lives when we have a purpose. We don't need to *rust* out; we need to *wear* out. Andrew is so thankful he has a purpose that is going to keep him going until he draws his last breath.

14a. *Discussion question:* Discuss some of the reasons people resist change.
   Discussion question
14b. What is true when you have a purpose?
   A. You will be happier
   B. You will be more productive
   C. Everything will work better in your life
   D. All of the above
   E. None of the above
   D. All of the above
14c. You don't need to _____ out; you need to _____ out.
   Rust / wear

15.   God will call us to do something beyond ourselves. This makes us dependent on Him. If we're just doing what we can do, we've missed God. If we really knew the plans that God has for us and what He wants to do with our lives, we would realize there's more than what we are doing. There are a satisfaction and a contentment that come when we know that we are doing what God called us to do.

> *I beseech you therefore, brethren, by the mercies of God, that ye present your bodies a living sacrifice, holy, acceptable unto God, which is your reasonable service. [2] And be not conformed to this world: but be ye transformed by the renewing of your mind, that ye may prove what is that good, and acceptable, and perfect, will of God.*
>
> ROMANS 12:1-2

This isn't just for full-time preachers or ministers—it's our normal Christian duty. Jesus died for us, so we should live for Him. We should commit ourselves without any questions. Let's take the limits off God, and we'll watch His blessings overtake us!

15a.   True or false: When God calls you to do something beyond yourself, it makes you more dependent on Him.
       True

15b.   A _____ and a _____ come when you know that you are doing what God has called you to do.
       Satisfaction / contentment

15c.   Is Romans 12:1-2 just for full-time preachers or ministers?
       No

15d.   *Discussion question:* What does "Jesus died for you, so you should live for Him" mean to you?
       Discussion question

LESSON 3.2 • FEAR OF RISK

DISCIPLESHIP QUESTIONS

16. Why do people fear that they will make mistakes?

_____

_____

_____

17. *Discussion question:* Why is it so important to find your security and identity in your relationship with God?

_____

_____

_____

18. *Discussion question:* When you get old, will you just sit around and wait on death?

_____

_____

_____

19. By telling God "I'll go anywhere or do anything You want," what will you bring into your life?
    A. Excitement
    B. Trouble
    C. Resistance
    D. All of the above
    E. None of the above

20. True or false: Being perfect means you are sinless.

21. In 2 Chronicles 16:9, God was referring to people who are _____ to Him.

22. What are some fears that may be limiting you and limiting what God can do?
    A. You may not prosper as much as you are now
    B. People may criticize you
    C. Something negative might happen
    D. All of the above
    E. None of the above

23. For the vast majority of people, where does their potential end up?

_____

_____

_____

24. Why do most people die without realizing their full potential?

_____

_____

_____

25. If you don't know what God put you here for, aren't doing what God has equipped you to do, and aren't reaching your full potential, is that living?

_____

_____

_____

26. *Discussion question:* In what ways should your life be touching others and making a difference?

_____

_____

_____

27. *Discussion question:* Discuss some of the reasons people resist change.

_____

_____

_____

28. What is true when you have a purpose?
    A. You will be happier
    B. You will be more productive
    C. Everything will work better in your life
    D. All of the above
    E. None of the above

29. You don't need to _____ out; you need to _____ out.

30. True or false: When God calls you to do something beyond yourself, it makes you more dependent on Him.

31. A _____ and a _____ come when you know that you are doing what God has called you to do.

32. Is Romans 12:1-2 just for full-time preachers or ministers?

     _____

     _____

     _____

33. *Discussion question:* What does "Jesus died for you, so you should live for Him" mean to you?

     _____

     _____

     _____

LESSON 3.2 • FEAR OF RISK

ANSWER KEY

16. They aren't secure in Jesus
17. *Discussion question*
18. *Discussion question*
19. A. Excitement
20. False
21. Committed
22. D. All of the above
23. In the grave
24. They set aside their dreams and goals—they let life limit them
25. No, it's just surviving
26. *Discussion question*
27. *Discussion question*
28. D. All of the above
29. Rust / wear
30. True
31. Satisfaction / contentment
32. No
33. *Discussion question*

LESSON 3.2 • FEAR OF RISK

SCRIPTURES

PROVERBS 24:16

For a just man falleth seven times, and riseth up again: but the wicked shall fall into mischief.

2 CHRONICLES 16:9

For the eyes of the LORD run to and fro throughout the whole earth, to shew himself strong in the behalf of them whose heart is perfect toward him. Herein thou hast done foolishly: therefore from henceforth thou shalt have wars.

PROVERBS 23:7

For as he thinketh in his heart, so is he: Eat and drink, saith he to thee; but his heart is not with thee.

ROMANS 12:1-2

I beseech you therefore, brethren, by the mercies of God, that ye present your bodies a living sacrifice, holy, acceptable unto God, which is your reasonable service. [2] And be not conformed to this world: but be ye transformed by the renewing of your mind, that ye may prove what is that good, and acceptable, and perfect, will of God.

FEAR OF MAN

When God spoke to me in 2002 and told me I was limiting Him, I realized I was doing so because of fear. There are many different types of fear that can hinder us and limit God. Fear activates Satan and releases his power the same way that faith activates God and releases His power. Fear paralyzes people. It is not a good thing. Yet many people are living their lives in fear.

One fear that limits what God can do in our lives is the fear of man—also known as persecution. One of the reasons I was limiting God in my life was because I had a fear of man; I was afraid of persecution.

If a certain dog bit you every time you bent over to pet it, after a while you would probably quit petting that dog. Nobody likes to be bitten. Nobody likes to be persecuted. If you enjoy people hating you, being mad at you, and saying bad things about you, then something is wrong with you. God created us for relationship and fellowship.

Enjoying hatred, strife, and persecution is not normal. If someone goes through life glorying in rubbing people the wrong way, something is wrong with that person. It's not normal or natural for us to like people hating and criticizing us. I don't like people being mad at me, but I've come to the place where I can overcome it and it won't keep me from doing what God's called me to do. I just cast my cares about it on the Lord (1 Pet. 5:7).

FLYING BELOW THE RADAR

When the Lord spoke to me about limiting Him, we were covering about 5 percent of the U.S. market with our television program. We were reaching people, and good things were happening; but we were flying below the radar. No one really zeroed in on me because I wasn't that big of a deal. I was enjoying my anonymity and enjoying not being criticized.

I knew that if I fulfilled what God told me to do and became a major player in the body of Christ—someone who was really influencing others—there was going to be persecution. I wasn't looking forward to this, so I was dog-paddling instead of swimming. I was content just floating along, instead of pursuing what God called me to do.

When you start doing what God called you to do, you have a huge target drawn on your back. Increased influence comes with increased criticism. When someone gets promoted into a leadership position, they will be picked apart with a fine-tooth comb. People will put a magnifying glass on that person and analyze and criticize everything they do. That's why most people would rather stay in the background. They don't want to face the criticism and persecution that go along with stepping out and doing what God called them to do. But this fear of persecution will limit what God can do in their lives.

FEAR OF MAN BRINGS A SNARE

I always tell our Bible college students that if they came to Bible college looking for something wrong, we have something for them. We are people; we aren't perfect. If someone comes and picks us apart, they will find something to criticize. The easiest way for most people to look good is by tearing others down and criticizing them. That's just human nature.

> *The fear of man bringeth a snare: but whoso putteth his trust in the LORD shall be safe.*
> PROVERBS 29:25

The vast majority of Christians are insecure because they are so paranoid about somebody criticizing them. For instance, many ministers won't speak the truth about what the Word of God says, because it's not politically correct. If we are so insecure that we can't handle another person criticizing us, we will never see God's fullness in our lives. We will limit God's plan for us.

But this insecurity is real even for those who are not preachers. There are other, subtle ways in which they can limit God. For instance, if our coworkers are talking about something that completely violates everything we believe in, most of us probably would not stand up for the truth because we are afraid of criticism and persecution. Although they wouldn't physically beat us up, they would look at us and roll their eyes. They wouldn't include us in their inner circle. They may even begin to avoid us. Yet most Christians will not speak the truth because it's politically incorrect. This is the fear of man, and it will limit God.

STAND UP FOR THE TRUTH

And Elijah the Tishbite, who was of the inhabitants of Gilead, said unto Ahab, As the LORD God of Israel liveth, before whom I stand, there shall not be dew nor rain these years, but according to my word.

1 KINGS 17:1

Elijah stood up in front of a king who was killing all of God's prophets. He walked right up to him and said, "Thus saith the Lord." Elijah identified himself with God, knowing that being one of God's ministers, he could be killed. Yet Elijah boldly walked up in front of all the people and said, "Thus saith the Lord, 'It will not rain until I say so.'" Since Elijah was bold enough to speak the truth, within three years, he was the central figure of that entire nation. The king was taking orders from Elijah because he stood up and spoke the truth.

Thou shalt not hate thy brother in thine heart: thou shalt in any wise rebuke thy neighbour, and not suffer sin upon him.

LEVITICUS 19:17

Most people won't stand up and speak for morality when people talk about shacking up with each other and acting like dogs and alley cats. We should stand up and say, "Did you know that's destructive? You need to make a commitment. Why would you want to live with someone who's not even committed to you?" One of the main reasons people shack up instead of making a commitment through marriage is so that the first time something goes wrong, they can leave without any encumbrances.

We will limit what God can do through us if we know something is true but won't stand up for the truth because we are afraid of what people will say. There is zero excuse for this in America. In foreign countries, many have given their lives standing up for the truth. That's true persecution! But in our country, we feel persecuted if people just look at us a certain way. We have become addicted to everyone's acceptance. We receive our ego boosts and acceptance from others, so we become codependent on people. We need our spouses', coworkers', children's, in-laws', or out-laws' approval. I'm not saying we should enjoy the rejection of others, but we should get to a place where if God loves us—which He does—then that ought to be sufficient for us. When we have a fear of man and let criticism and rejection keep us from doing what God called us to do, we limit Him.

GOD IS ENOUGH

I have a Scandinavian friend who was ministering in Africa and had started some churches there. He was really struggling because it seemed like nothing was working for him. One day he was out in the jungle complaining about how nobody loved him and how people hadn't accepted him. All of a sudden, the Lord spoke to him in such a loud voice that the ground shook. He could actually see the trees swaying as God asked, "Walter, aren't I enough?"

Needless to say, Walter repented. When he realized he had been limiting God because of a fear of man, he stopped complaining and instead planted over 500 churches in Africa! We all need to stop limiting God in our lives and get to the place where God is enough. It's amazing how insecure we become when we aren't in a vibrant relationship with God. We need to have everyone else's approval. The only people who will ever let us down are those whom we lean on. If we don't lean on anyone but Jesus, nobody can let us down.

If the Lord tells us to move to Africa or someplace else and we stop to consider what our family or others would think, we have a fear of man. I'm not saying we shouldn't be thinking about these things or that we should present what has God said in a way that's offensive. But for us to debate whether we're going to do what God tells us to do because someone might not like it is a fear of man.

As a minister, I've had to deal with this a lot. I don't like it when people hate me or spit in my face—nobody does. One thing that really helped me was when the Lord instructed me to tell someone something that I knew this person didn't want to hear. I knew they weren't going to like it, so I was debating whether or not to say anything. Finally, the Lord spoke to me and said that I had no right to reject the truth for this person. He told me that we need to give people the right to reject His Word on their own. This changed my thinking, as I realized that when we don't tell people the truth because we're afraid of how they might respond, we reject the truth for them.

LESSON 4.1 • FEAR OF MAN
OUTLINE

I. Fear activates Satan and releases his power the same way that faith activates God and releases His power.
  A. Fear paralyzes people, yet many people are living their lives in fear.
  B. One fear that limits what God can do in our lives is the fear of man, also known as persecution.
  C. Nobody likes to be persecuted.
  D. God created us for relationship and fellowship.
  E. It's not normal or natural for us to like people hating or criticizing us.
  F. But we can cast our cares about it on the Lord (1 Pet. 5:7).

II. When you start doing what God called you to do, you have a huge target drawn on your back.
  A. Increased influence comes with increased criticism.
  B. That's why most people would rather stay in the background.
  C. They don't want to face the criticism and persecution that go along with stepping out and doing what God called them to do.

III. The vast majority of Christians are insecure because they are so paranoid about somebody criticizing them.

  The fear of man bringeth a snare: but whoso putteth his trust in the Lord shall be safe.
  PROVERBS 29:25

  A. If we are so insecure that we can't handle another person criticizing us, we will never see God's fullness in our lives.

  And Elijah the Tishbite, who was of the inhabitants of Gilead, said unto Ahab, As the Lord God of Israel liveth, before whom I stand, there shall not be dew nor rain these years, but according to my word.
  1 KINGS 17:1

  B. Elijah stood up in front of a king who was killing all of God's prophets, knowing that he himself could be killed.
  C. He was bold enough to speak the truth.
  D. We will limit what God can do through us if we know something is true but won't stand up for the truth because we are afraid of what people will say.

    E. We have become addicted to everyone's acceptance.

    F. It's not that we should enjoy the rejection of others, but we should get to a place where if God loves us—which He does—then that ought to be sufficient for us.

IV.   It's amazing how insecure we become when we aren't in a vibrant relationship with God—we need to have everyone else's approval.

    A. For us to debate whether we're going to do what God tells us to do because someone might not like it is a fear of man.

    B. We have no right to reject the truth for other people.

    C. We need to give people the right to reject His Word on their own.

    D. When we don't tell people the truth because we're afraid of how they might respond, we reject the truth for them.

LESSON 4.1 • FEAR OF MAN
TEACHER'S GUIDE

1.   Fear activates Satan and releases his power the same way that faith activates God and releases His power. Fear paralyzes people, yet many people are living their lives in fear. One fear that limits what God can do in our lives is the fear of man, also known as persecution. Nobody likes to be persecuted. God created us for relationship and fellowship. It's not normal or natural for us to like people hating or criticizing us. But we can cast our cares about it on the Lord (1 Pet. 5:7).

1a.   True or false: Fear activates Satan and releases his power the same way that faith activates God and releases His power.
True
1b.   What is another name for persecution?
Fear of man
1c.   *Discussion question:* Why do you think no one likes to be persecuted?
Discussion question

2.   When we start doing what God called us to do, we have huge targets drawn on our backs. Increased influence comes with increased criticism. That's why most people would rather stay in the background. They don't want to face the criticism and persecution that go along with stepping out and doing what God called them to do.

2a.   Increased _____ comes with increased _____.
Influence / criticism
2b.   Why do most people stay in the background?
They don't want to face the criticism and persecution that go along with stepping out and doing what God called them to do

3.   The vast majority of Christians are insecure because they are so paranoid about somebody criticizing them.

> *The fear of man bringeth a snare: but whoso putteth his trust in the Lord shall be safe.*
>
> PROVERBS 29:25

If we are so insecure that we can't handle another person criticizing us, we will never see God's fullness in our lives.

> *And Elijah the Tishbite, who was of the inhabitants of Gilead, said unto Ahab, As the Lord God of Israel liveth, before whom I stand, there shall not be dew nor rain these years, but according to my word.*
>
> 1 KINGS 17:1

Elijah stood up in front of a king who was killing all of God's prophets, knowing that he himself could be killed. He was bold enough to speak the truth. We will limit what God can do through us if we know something is true but won't stand up for the truth because we are afraid of what people will say. We have become addicted to everyone's acceptance. It's not that we should enjoy the rejection of others, but we should get to a place where if God loves us—which He does—then that ought to be sufficient for us.

3a.   Proverbs 29:25 says, *"The fear of man bringeth a _____: but whoso putteth his trust in the Lord shall be safe."*
      "Snare"
3b.   *Discussion question:* What lessons can you learn from Elijah's boldness?
      Discussion question
3c.   If God loves you—which He does—then that ought to be what?
      A. A point on your spiritual scorecard
      B. Sufficient for you
      C. Good for a free drink at the coffee shop
      D. All of the above
      E. None of the above
      B. Sufficient for you

4.   It's amazing how insecure we become when we aren't in a vibrant relationship with God—we need to have everyone else's approval. For us to debate whether we're going to do what God tells us to do because someone might not like it is a fear of man. We have no right to reject the truth for other people. We need to give people the right to reject His Word on their own. When we don't tell people the truth because we're afraid of how they might respond, we reject the truth for them.

4a.   True or false: For you to debate whether you're going to do what God tells you to do because someone might not like it is a fear of failure.
      False
4b.   *Discussion question:* Discuss why you have no right to reject the truth for other people.
      Discussion question

LESSON 4.1 • FEAR OF MAN
DISCIPLESHIP QUESTIONS

1. True or false: Fear activates Satan and releases his power the same way that faith activates God and releases His power.

2. What is another name for persecution?

   _____

   _____

   _____

3. *Discussion question:* Why do you think no one likes to be persecuted?

   _____

   _____

   _____

4. Increased _____ comes with increased _____.

5. Why do most people stay in the background?

   _____

   _____

   _____

6. Proverbs 29:25 says, *"The fear of man bringeth a _____: but whoso putteth his trust in the LORD shall be safe."*

7. *Discussion question:* What lessons can you learn from Elijah's boldness?

   _____

   _____

   _____

8.   If God loves you—which He does—then that ought to be what?
     A. A point on your spiritual scorecard
     B. Sufficient for you
     C. Good for a free drink at the coffee shop
     D. All of the above
     E. None of the above

9.   True or false: For you to debate whether you're going to do what God tells you to do because someone might not like it is a fear of failure.

10. *Discussion question:* Discuss why you have no right to reject the truth for other people.

     _____

     _____

     _____

LESSON 4.1 • FEAR OF MAN
ANSWER KEY

1. True
2. Fear of man
3. *Discussion question*
4. Influence / criticism
5. They don't want to face the criticism and persecution that go along with stepping out and doing what God called them to do
6. *"Snare"*
7. *Discussion question*
8. B. Sufficient for you
9. False
10. *Discussion question*

LESSON 4.1 • FEAR OF MAN
SCRIPTURES

1 PETER 5:7
Casting all your care upon him; for he careth for you.

PROVERBS 29:25
The fear of man bringeth a snare: but whoso putteth his trust in the LORD shall be safe.

1 KINGS 17:1
And Elijah the Tishbite, who was of the inhabitants of Gilead, said unto Ahab, As the LORD God of Israel liveth, before whom I stand, there shall not be dew nor rain these years, but according to my word.

LEVITICUS 19:17
Thou shalt not hate thy brother in thine heart: thou shalt in any wise rebuke thy neighbour, and not suffer sin upon him.

FEAR OF MAN

Many people are afraid someone is going to criticize them or reject them, so they are paralyzed and unable to do what God tells them to do. Once, in one of my meetings, hundreds of people raised their hands when asked if they would go to Bible college if they had no restraints. Some common restraints people have are the thoughts: *What would my family think? What would a particular person think? People are going to think I've lost my mind.* All of this is a fear of man, which will limit God.

> *The fear of man bringeth a snare: but whoso putteth his trust in the LORD shall be safe.*
> PROVERBS 29:25

Some people who have come to our Bible college, however, have not allowed such restraints to stop them. There was one woman from Utah whose husband told her that he would divorce her if she got on the plane to come to our Bible college. Their marriage was already in trouble, so she came anyway—and he divorced her. Because of situations like this, people become paralyzed and don't obey what God tells them to do.

We need to come to a place where, when God speaks to us, nobody else is going to stop us from doing what He told us to do. Fear of man will bring bondage into our lives, so we need to get over it! We cannot respect or honor anyone else's opinion as much as we honor God's opinion.

THE ISRAELITES LIMITED GOD

And they ascended by the south, and came unto Hebron; where Ahiman, Sheshai, and Talmai, the children of Anak, were. (Now Hebron was built seven years before Zoan in Egypt.) [23] And they came unto the brook of Eshcol, and cut down from thence a branch with one cluster of grapes, and they bare it between two upon a staff; and they brought of the pomegranates, and of the figs. [24] The place was called the brook Eshcol, because of the cluster of grapes which the children of Israel cut down from thence. [25] And they returned from searching of the land after forty days. [26] And they went and came to Moses, and to

Aaron, and to all the congregation of the children of Israel, unto the wilderness of Paran, to Kadesh; and brought back word unto them, and unto all the congregation, and shewed them the fruit of the land. [27] And they told him, and said, We came unto the land whither thou sentest us, and surely it floweth with milk and honey; and this is the fruit of it. [28] Nevertheless the people be strong that dwell in the land, and the cities are walled, and very great: and moreover we saw the children of Anak there. [29] The Amalekites dwell in the land of the south: and the Hittites, and the Jebusites, and the Amorites, dwell in the mountains: and the Canaanites dwell by the sea, and by the coast of Jordan. [30] And Caleb stilled the people before Moses, and said, Let us go up at once, and possess it; for we are well able to overcome it. [31] But the men that went up with him said, We be not able to go up against the people; for they are stronger than we. [32] And they brought up an evil report of the land which they had searched unto the children of Israel, saying, The land, through which we have gone to search it, is a land that eateth up the inhabitants thereof; and all the people that we saw in it are men of a great stature. [33] And there we saw the giants, the sons of Anak, which come of the giants: and we were in our own sight as grasshoppers, and so we were in their sight.

NUMBERS 13:22-33

God wanted the Israelites to enter into the Promised Land—a land that flowed with milk and honey. It was lush! A cluster of grapes was so big, it had to be placed on a pole and carried between two men. Can you imagine a cluster of grapes that large? These weren't like the grapes we have today. These grapes were huge! That's how blessed this land was!

But the Israelites focused their attention on the wrong thing. They looked at the size of the inhabitants rather than the land that God told them to possess. They saw the people as giants and themselves as grasshoppers. But it doesn't matter how other people see us; it matters how God sees us. And we need to see ourselves as God sees us!

GOD'S WILL DELAYED

Forty years later, Joshua sent new spies into Jericho. Rahab, the harlot, took the spies in and hid them from the king. Then she asked the spies to have mercy upon her and upon her household when the Israelites conquered Jericho.

And she said unto the men, I know that the LORD hath given you the land, and that your terror is fallen upon us, and that all the inhabitants of the land faint because of you. [10] For we have heard how the LORD dried up the water of the Red sea for you, when ye came out of Egypt; and what ye did unto the two kings of the Amorites, that were on the other side Jordan, Sihon and Og, whom ye utterly destroyed. [11] And as soon as we had heard these things, our hearts did melt, neither did there remain any more courage in any man, because of you: for the LORD your God, he is God in heaven above, and in earth beneath. [12] Now therefore, I pray you, swear unto me by the LORD, since I have shewed you kindness, that ye will also shew kindness unto my father's house, and give me a true token: [13] And that ye will save alive my father, and my mother, and my brethren, and my sisters, and all that they have, and deliver our lives from death. [14] And the men answered her, Our life for yours, if ye utter not this our business. And it shall be, when the LORD hath given us the land, that we will deal kindly and truly with thee. [15] Then she let them down by a cord through the window: for her house was upon the town wall, and she dwelt upon the wall. [16] And she said unto them, Get you to the mountain, lest the pursuers meet you; and hide yourselves there three days, until the pursuers be returned: and afterward may ye go your way. [17] And the men said unto her, We will be blameless of this thine oath which thou hast made us swear. [18] Behold, when we come into the land, thou shalt bind this line of scarlet thread in the window which thou didst let us down by: and thou shalt bring thy father, and thy mother, and thy brethren, and all thy father's household, home unto thee. [19] And it shall be, that whosoever shall go out of the doors of thy house into the street, his blood shall be upon his head, and we will be guiltless: and whosoever shall be with thee in the house, his blood shall be on our head, if any hand be upon him. [20] And if thou utter this our business, then we will be quit of thine oath which thou hast made us to swear. [21] And she said, According unto your words, so be it. And she sent them away, and they departed: and she bound the scarlet line in the window. [22] And they went, and came unto the mountain, and abode there three days, until the pursuers were returned: and the pursuers sought them throughout all the way, but found them not. [23] So the two men returned, and descended from the mountain, and passed over, and came to Joshua the son of Nun, and told him all things that befell them: [24] And they said unto Joshua, Truly the LORD hath delivered into our hands all the land; for even all the inhabitants of the country do faint because of us.

JOSHUA 2:9-24

Yes, they were great men of stature! Yes, they were giants! But this tells us what they were thinking. For forty years, they had been fearful of the Israelites. Their hearts had melted, and their strength had left them. If the Israelites had analyzed their situation properly, it would have been a cakewalk for them to go into the Promised Land. God would have given them total victory. But instead, they looked at the size of the people and saw them as giants. By focusing their attention on the natural instead of obeying God, they delayed His plan from coming to pass for forty years. They limited God!

UNCIRCUMCISED PHILISTINE

Let's contrast this with 1 Samuel 17, where David went out to face Goliath. While the rest of the mighty men were all hiding behind rocks because they were afraid of the giant, David looked at Goliath and said, *"Who is this uncircumcised Philistine?"* (1 Sam. 17:26). David was talking about the covenant of circumcision. Goliath was not an Israelite; he was not one of God's covenant people.

This would be equivalent to us saying, "Who is this person—who doesn't even have a covenant with God and isn't one of God's people—to stand against those who are God's people?" This is the same attitude we ought to have when unbelievers criticize us. It doesn't matter whether they are family members, friends, coworkers, or persons in positions of authority. If they don't know God, then our opinion of God is better than their opinion of God. After all, their opinion is sending them to hell!

If we are born again and have the baptism of the Holy Spirit, we are the exception today. When we receive the baptism of the Holy Spirit, we have a revelation of God and an access to Him that a lot of Christians don't have. If we are born again and Spirit filled, we are an elite group already. Why in the world would we elevate someone else's opinion and put that kind of authority upon someone who doesn't even have a relationship with God?

THE GODLY WILL SUFFER PERSECUTION

Nobody can intimidate us without our consent or cooperation. Nobody can have influence over us unless we give it to them. If we are worried about what someone is going to say about us, it's because we have a fear of man, instead of a fear of God. Or perhaps, our fear of man is greater than our fear of God. When we let a fear of man determine what we do, it's actually an indication of a deficiency in us—not in them. It's not the people who criticize us who are the problem; we are the problem.

If we throw a rock into a pack of dogs, the dog that yelps the loudest is the one who got hit. In the same way, when we take a stand for the Lord, the one who criticizes us the most is under the most conviction. People try to deal with conviction by tearing us down and discrediting us because if they can cause us to fall apart, they can then say, "See, I was right."

In court, if a witness has a damaging testimony, the lawyer will assault the witness's character. If the lawyer can make that witness appear to have a poor character, then their testimony will be dismissed. That's what persecution is all about!

> *For every one that doeth evil hateth the light, neither cometh to the light, lest his deeds should be reproved.*
>
> JOHN 3:20

If we take a moral stand on social issues, immoral people will criticize us. Our morality will condemn them. This doesn't mean that we condemn them. All people, at a heart level, know when they are wrong. They don't like the sense of guilt and condemnation, so when we stand up for the values they are against, they will attack us in an attempt to make themselves look good. They want to dim the light of others so it won't shine on their sin. That's the reason criticism comes. If we understood this, we would realize that being criticized and persecuted is actually a compliment.

> *And all that will live godly in Christ Jesus shall suffer persecution.*
>
> 2 TIMOTHY 3:12

If we aren't suffering persecution, we aren't living godly. If nobody says anything critical about us, we are not being good Christians or ministering the Word properly. Jesus said, *"Remember the word that I said unto you, The servant is not greater than his lord. If they have persecuted me, they will also persecute you; if they have kept my saying, they will keep yours also"* (John 15:20). In other words, if the master of the house received criticism, we will too!

I've gotten to where I just rest in God, knowing that He loves me. Then when criticism and persecution come, they will not detract or stop me from doing what God told me to do. I've got hundreds, maybe thousands, of blogs written about me on the internet saying that I'm a terrible person. People say all kinds of things about me, but that isn't going to change me.

Fear of man and fear of persecution paralyze a lot of people. Most people are so frail, they are not willing to take persecution. This is indicative of not having a relationship with God. When they want the praises of man more than the praises of God, they limit God.

LESSON 4.2 • FEAR OF MAN
OUTLINE

V. Many people are afraid someone is going to criticize them or reject them, so they are paralyzed and unable to do what God tells them to do.
    A. All of this is a fear of man, which will limit God.

    The fear of man bringeth a snare: but whoso putteth his trust in the LORD shall be safe.
    PROVERBS 29:25

    B. We need to come to a place where, when God speaks to us, nobody else is going to stop us from doing what He told us to do.
    C. We cannot respect or honor anyone else's opinion as much as we honor God's opinion.

VI. God wanted the Israelites to enter into the Promised Land, but the Israelites focused their attention on the wrong thing (Num. 13:22-33).
    A. They looked at the size of the inhabitants rather than the land that God told them to possess—they saw the people as giants and themselves as grasshoppers.
    B. It doesn't matter how other people see us; it matters how God sees us.
    C. We need to see ourselves as God sees us!
    D. If the Israelites had analyzed their situation properly, it would have been a cakewalk for them to go into the Promised Land (Josh. 2:9-24).
    E. By focusing their attention on the natural instead of obeying God, they delayed His plan from coming to pass for forty years.

VII. In 1 Samuel 17, David went out to face Goliath and said, *"Who is this uncircumcised Philistine?"* (1 Sam. 17:26).
    A. Goliath was not an Israelite; he was not one of God's covenant people.
    B. We ought to have this same attitude when unbelievers criticize us.
    C. If they don't know God, then our opinion of God is better than their opinion of God.
    D. If we are born again and have the baptism of the Holy Spirit, we are the exception today: We have a revelation of God and an access to Him that a lot of Christians don't have.
    E. Why would we elevate someone else's opinion and put that kind of authority upon someone who doesn't even have a relationship with God?

VIII. When we take a stand for the Lord, the one who criticizes us the most is under the most conviction.
    A. People try to deal with conviction by tearing us down and discrediting us.
    B. If a witness appears to have a poor character, then their testimony will be dismissed—that's what persecution is all about!

> *For every one that doeth evil hateth the light, neither cometh to the light, lest his deeds should be reproved.*
>
> JOHN 3:20

    C. Immoral people want to dim the light of others so it won't shine on their sin—that's the reason criticism comes.

> *And all that will live godly in Christ Jesus shall suffer persecution.*
>
> 2 TIMOTHY 3:12

    D. If we aren't suffering persecution, we aren't living godly.
    E. Jesus said, *"Remember the word that I said unto you, The servant is not greater than his lord. If they have persecuted me, they will also persecute you; if they have kept my saying, they will keep yours also"* (John 15:20).
    F. When people want the praises of man more than the praises of God, they limit God.

LESSON 4.2 • FEAR OF MAN
TEACHER'S GUIDE

5.   Many people are afraid someone is going to criticize them or reject them, so they are paralyzed and unable to do what God tells them to do. All of this is a fear of man, which will limit God.

> *The fear of man bringeth a snare: but whoso putteth his trust in the L*ORD *shall be safe.*
> PROVERBS 29:25

We need to come to a place where, when God speaks to us, nobody else is going to stop us from doing what He told us to do. We cannot respect or honor anyone else's opinion as much as we honor God's opinion.

5a.   *Discussion question:* In what ways have you let fear of criticism or rejection paralyze you and keep you from doing what God tells you to do?
Discussion question

5b.   You cannot _____ or _____ anyone else's opinion as much as you honor God's opinion.
Respect / honor

6.   God wanted the Israelites to enter into the Promised Land, but the Israelites focused their attention on the wrong thing (Num. 13:22-33). They looked at the size of the inhabitants rather than the land that God told them to possess—they saw the people as giants and themselves as grasshoppers. It doesn't matter how other people see us; it matters how God sees us. We need to see ourselves as God sees us! If the Israelites had analyzed their situation properly, it would have been a cakewalk for them to go into the Promised Land (Josh. 2:9-24). By focusing their attention on the natural instead of obeying God, they delayed His plan from coming to pass for forty years.

6a.   *Discussion question:* How can focusing on the wrong thing affect God's plan for you, like it did the Israelites in the wilderness?
    Discussion question

6b.   What were the Israelites looking at that kept them out of the land God told them to possess?
    A.   The size of their weapons
    B.   The size of their wallets
    C.   The size of the inhabitants
    D.   The size of their problems
    E.   The size of the land
    C.   The size of the inhabitants

6c.   True or false: If the Israelites had analyzed their situation properly, it would have been very difficult for them to go into the Promised Land.
    False

7.   In 1 Samuel 17, David went out to face Goliath and said, *"Who is this uncircumcised Philistine?"* (1 Sam. 17:26). Goliath was not an Israelite; he was not one of God's covenant people. We ought to have this same attitude when unbelievers criticize us. If they don't know God, then our opinion of God is better than their opinion of God. If we are born again and have the baptism of the Holy Spirit, we are the exception today: We have a revelation of God and an access to Him that a lot of Christians don't have. Why would we elevate someone else's opinion and put that kind of authority upon someone who doesn't even have a relationship with God?

7a.   *Discussion question:* Why should David's attitude toward Goliath be the same attitude you have toward unbelievers who criticize you?
    Discussion question

7b.   If you are born again and baptized in the Holy Spirit, you have a _____ of God and an _____ to Him that a lot of Christians don't.
    Revelation / access

7c.   *Discussion question:* Why do you think some believers elevate the opinion of others and put that kind of authority upon people who don't even have a relationship with God?
    Discussion question

8.   When we take a stand for the Lord, the one who criticizes us the most is under the most conviction. People try to deal with conviction by tearing us down and discrediting us. If a witness appears to have a poor character, then their testimony will be dismissed—that's what persecution is all about!

> *For every one that doeth evil hateth the light, neither cometh to the light, lest his deeds should be reproved.*
>
> JOHN 3:20

Immoral people want to dim the light of others so it won't shine on their sin—that's the reason criticism comes.

> *And all that will live godly in Christ Jesus shall suffer persecution.*
>
> 2 TIMOTHY 3:12

If we aren't suffering persecution, we aren't living godly. Jesus said, *"Remember the word that I said unto you, The servant is not greater than his lord. If they have persecuted me, they will also persecute you; if they have kept my saying, they will keep yours also"* (John 15:20). When people want the praises of man more than the praises of God, they limit God.

8a.   When you take a stand, the person who criticizes you is what?
    A. The noisiest
    B. Under the most conviction
    C. Running for political office
    D. One of your relatives
    E. Just being mean
    B. Under the most conviction
8b.   For what reason does criticism come?
    Immoral people don't want the light of others to shine on their sin (John 3:20)
8c.   *Discussion question:* How can desiring the praises of man limit God?
    Discussion question

LESSON 4.2 • FEAR OF MAN
DISCIPLESHIP QUESTIONS

11. *Discussion question:* In what ways have you let fear of criticism or rejection paralyze you and keep you from doing what God tells you to do?

   _____

   _____

   _____

12. You cannot _____ or _____ anyone else's opinion as much as you honor God's opinion.

13. *Discussion question:* How can focusing on the wrong thing affect God's plan for you, like it did the Israelites in the wilderness?

   _____

   _____

   _____

14. What were the Israelites looking at that kept them out of the land God told them to possess?
    A. The size of their weapons
    B. The size of their wallets
    C. The size of the inhabitants
    D. The size of their problems
    E. The size of the land

15. True or false: If the Israelites had analyzed their situation properly, it would have been very difficult for them to go into the Promised Land.

16. *Discussion question:* Why should David's attitude toward Goliath be the same attitude you have toward unbelievers who criticize you?

   _____

   _____

   _____

17. If you are born again and baptized in the Holy Spirit, you have a _____ of God and an _____ to Him that a lot of Christians don't.

18. *Discussion question:* Why do you think some believers elevate the opinion of others and put that kind of authority upon people who don't even have a relationship with God?

_____

_____

_____

19. When you take a stand, the person who criticizes you is what?
    A. The noisiest
    B. Under the most conviction
    C. Running for political office
    D. One of your relatives
    E. Just being mean

20. For what reason does criticism come?

_____

_____

_____

21. *Discussion question:* How can desiring the praises of man limit God?

_____

_____

_____

LESSON 4.2 • FEAR OF MAN

ANSWER KEY

11. *Discussion question*
12. Respect / honor
13. *Discussion question*
14. C. The size of the inhabitants
15. False
16. *Discussion question*
17. Revelation / access
18. *Discussion question*
19. B. Under the most conviction
20. Immoral people don't want the light of others to shine on their sin (John 3:20)
21. *Discussion question*

LESSON 4.2 • FEAR OF MAN

SCRIPTURES

PROVERBS 29:25

The fear of man bringeth a snare: but whoso putteth his trust in the LORD shall be safe.

NUMBERS 13:22-33

And they ascended by the south, and came unto Hebron; where Ahiman, Sheshai, and Talmai, the children of Anak, were. (Now Hebron was built seven years before Zoan in Egypt.) [23] And they came unto the brook of Eshcol, and cut down from thence a branch with one cluster of grapes, and they bare it between two upon a staff; and they brought of the pomegranates, and of the figs. [24] The place was called the brook Eshcol, because of the cluster of grapes which the children of Israel cut down from thence. [25] And they returned from searching of the land after forty days. [26] And they went and came to Moses, and to Aaron, and to all the congregation of the children of Israel, unto the wilderness of Paran, to Kadesh; and brought back word unto them, and unto all the congregation, and shewed them the fruit of the land. [27] And they told him, and said, We came unto the land whither thou sentest us, and surely it floweth with milk and honey; and this is the fruit of it. [28] Nevertheless the people be strong that dwell in the land, and the cities are walled, and very great: and moreover we saw the children of Anak there. [29] The Amalekites dwell in the land of the south: and the Hittites, and the Jebusites, and the Amorites, dwell in the mountains: and the Canaanites dwell by the sea, and by the coast of Jordan. [30] And Caleb stilled the people before Moses, and said, Let us go up at once, and possess it; for we are well able to overcome it. [31] But the men that went up with him said, We be not able to go up against the people; for they are stronger than we. [32] And they brought up an evil report of the land which they had searched unto the children of Israel, saying, The land, through which we have gone to search it, is a land that eateth up the inhabitants thereof; and all the people that we saw in it are men of a great stature. [33] And there we saw the giants, the sons of Anak, which come of the giants: and we were in our own sight as grasshoppers, and so we were in their sight.

JOSHUA 2:9-24

And she said unto the men, I know that the LORD hath given you the land, and that your terror is fallen upon us, and that all the inhabitants of the land faint because of you. [10] For we have heard how the LORD dried up the water of the Red sea for you, when ye came out of Egypt; and what ye did unto the two kings of the Amorites, that were on the other side Jordan, Sihon and Og, whom ye utterly destroyed. [11] And as soon as we had heard these things, our hearts did melt, neither did there remain any more courage in any man, because of you: for the LORD your God, he is God in heaven above, and in earth beneath. [**12**] Now therefore, I pray you, swear unto me by the L ORD, since I have shewed you kindness, that ye will also shew kindness unto my father's house, and give me a true token: [**13**] And that ye will save alive my father, and my mother, and my brethren, and my sisters, and all that they have, and deliver our lives from death. [**14**] And the men answered her, Our life for yours, if ye utter not this our business. And it shall be, when the L ORD hath given us the land, that we will deal kindly and truly with thee. [**15**] Then she let them down by a cord through the window: for her house was upon the town wall, and she dwelt upon the wall. [**16**] And she said unto them, Get you to the mountain, lest the pursuers meet you; and hide yourselves there three days, until the pursuers be returned: and afterward may ye go your way. [**17**] And the men said unto her, We will be blameless of this thine oath which thou hast made us swear. [**18**] Behold, when we come into the land, thou shalt bind this line of scarlet thread in the window which thou didst let us down by: and thou shalt bring thy father, and thy mother, and thy brethren, and all thy father's household, home unto thee. [**19**] And it shall be, that whosoever shall go out of the doors of thy house into the street, his blood shall be upon his head, and we will be guiltless: and whosoever shall be with thee in the house, his blood shall be on our head, if any hand be upon him. [**20**] And if thou utter this our business, then we will be quit of thine oath which thou hast made us to swear. [**21**] And she said, According unto your words, so be it. And she sent them away, and they departed: and she bound the scarlet line in the window. [**22**] And they went, and came unto the mountain, and abode there three days, until the pursuers were returned: and the pursuers sought them throughout all the way, but found them not. [**23**] So the two men returned, and descended from the mountain, and passed over, and came to Joshua the son of Nun, and told him all things that befell them: [**24**] And they said unto Joshua, Truly the L ORD hath delivered into our hands all the land; for even all the inhabitants of the country do faint because of us.

1 SAMUEL 17:26

And David spake to the men that stood by him, saying, What shall be done to the man that killeth this Philistine, and taketh away the reproach from Israel? for who is this uncircumcised Philistine, that he should defy the armies of the living God?

JOHN 3:20

For every one that doeth evil hateth the light, neither cometh to the light, lest his deeds should be reproved.

2 TIMOTHY 3:12

Yea, and all that will live godly in Christ Jesus shall suffer persecution.

JOHN 15:20

Remember the word that I said unto you, The servant is not greater than his lord. If they have persecuted me, they will also persecute you; if they have kept my saying, they will keep yours also.

DON'T LIMIT GOD

FEAR OF SUCCESS

When God spoke to me and told me I was limiting Him, one of the biggest fears in my life was the fear of success. Some of you don't understand what I'm saying, but I believe that success has destroyed more people than hardship and failure ever have. People often say things like, "When you're suffering and everything is wrong, it shows what's inside of you." But what really reveals what's inside of you is when everything is going well. Everyone, with even a minimal commitment to God, will turn to Him when things aren't working and it looks like they are going to die at any moment. Even people who don't love God will cry out to Him and ask Him for help when they are in a bind.

Two things have I required of thee; deny me them not before I die: [8] Remove far from me vanity and lies: give me neither poverty nor riches; feed me with food convenient for me: [9] Lest I be full, and deny thee, and say, Who is the Lord? or lest I be poor, and steal, and take the name of my God in vain.

PROVERBS 30:7-9

I believe that a greater indication of what's on the inside of you is when everything is going well and you don't have to rely on God. How much do you study and pray then?

DON'T FORGET THE LORD

All the commandments which I command thee this day shall ye observe to do, that ye may live, and multiply, and go in and possess the land which the Lord sware unto your fathers. [2] And thou shalt remember all the way which the Lord thy God led thee these forty years in the wilderness, to humble thee, and to prove thee, to know what was in thine heart, whether thou wouldest keep his commandments, or no. [3] And he humbled thee, and suffered thee to hunger, and fed thee with manna, which thou knewest not, neither did thy fathers know; that he might make thee know that man doth not live by bread only, but by every word that proceedeth out of the mouth of the Lord doth man live. [4] Thy raiment waxed not old upon thee, neither did thy foot swell, these forty years. [5] Thou shalt also consider in thine heart, that, as a man chasteneth his son, so the Lord thy God chasteneth thee. [6] Therefore thou shalt keep the commandments of the Lord thy God, to walk in his ways, and to fear him. [7] For the LORD thy God bringeth thee into a good land, a land of brooks of water, of fountains and depths that spring out of valleys and hills; [8] A land of wheat, and barley, and vines, and fig trees, and pomegranates; a land of oil olive, and honey; [9] A land wherein thou shalt eat bread without scarceness, thou shalt not lack any thing in it; a land whose stones are iron, and out of whose hills thou mayest dig brass. [10] When thou hast eaten and art full, then thou shalt bless the LORD thy God for the good land which he hath given thee. [11] Beware that thou forget not the LORD thy God, in not keeping his commandments, and his judgments, and his statutes, which I command thee this day: [12] Lest when thou hast eaten and art full, and hast built goodly houses, and dwelt therein; [13] And when thy herds and thy flocks multiply, and thy silver and thy gold is multiplied, and all that thou hast is multiplied; [14] Then thine heart be lifted up, and thou forget the LORD thy God, which brought thee forth out of the land of Egypt, from the house of bondage; [15] Who led thee through that great and terrible wilderness, wherein were fiery serpents, and scorpions, and drought, where there was no water; who brought thee forth water out of the rock of flint; [16] Who fed thee in the wilderness with manna, which thy fathers knew not, that he might humble thee, and that he might prove thee, to do thee good at thy latter end; [17] And thou say in thine heart, My power and the might of mine hand hath gotten me this wealth. [18] But thou shalt remember the LORD thy God: for it is he that giveth thee power to get wealth, that he may establish his covenant which he sware unto thy fathers, as it is this day. [19] And it shall be, if thou do at all forget the LORD thy God, and walk after other gods, and serve them, and worship them, I testify against you this day that ye shall surely perish. [20] As the nations which the LORD destroyeth before your face, so shall ye perish; because ye would not be obedient unto the voice of the Lord your God.

DEUTERONOMY 8:1-20

In this chapter, Moses was writing to the Israelites about entering into the Promised Land. He told them to beware that when they came into all of this prosperity, they didn't forget that it was the Lord who gave them the power to get wealth so He could establish His covenant. King Saul's life is a good example of this.

And Samuel said, When thou wast little in thine own sight, wast thou not made the head of the tribes of Israel, and the LORD anointed thee king over Israel?

1 SAMUEL 15:17

And Samuel said unto Saul, I will not return with thee: for thou hast rejected the word of the LORD, and the LORD hath rejected thee from being king over Israel.

1 SAMUEL 15:26

When Saul was little in his own eyes—was humble and obeyed God—God could use him. But when he became great in his own eyes—was lifted up with pride and disobeyed God—God couldn't use him.

Humility is necessary to walk with God. Saul didn't continue to walk with God, because he became proud and did his own thing. God rejected him from being king. Saul limited what God wanted to do in his life.

> *Pride goeth before destruction, and an haughty spirit before a fall.*
>
> PROVERBS 16:18

> *God resisteth the proud, and giveth grace to the humble.*
>
> 1 PETER 5:5

There is fear in prosperity. Prosperity has destroyed a lot of people and has hardened many people's hearts to the Lord. This is a problem in our nation today. America is so prosperous that we have spoiled people walking around who think if they don't have five flat-screen television sets, the government should do something about it!

If we look at church history, we can see that every time the church was persecuted, it flourished. But every time the church was in a relative period of prosperity, it always went into apostasy. I believe that's what is happening in our nation today. We have become religious. America was founded on Christian principles, but now the church has minimal impact in our nation. In a lot of ways—and I take no joy in saying this—we are living in a post-Christian nation. I am not accepting that, and I'm not dooming us to that conclusion. I believe God will still resurrect our nation, and I'm doing everything that I can by preaching the Word. I'm still believing God for our nation.

PRIDE COMES BEFORE A FALL

Proverbs 16:18 can also be applied to King Uzziah who was another king who started out serving God in humility. God gave him witty inventions, such as the engines he built that gave him military advances over his enemies. He prospered, but then he got lifted up with pride. He went into the temple and decided he was going to offer a sacrifice to God. He tried to occupy the priest's place, but a king couldn't do that. So, God smote him with leprosy.

> *And Uzziah prepared for them throughout all the host shields, and spears, and helmets, and habergeons, and bows, and slings to cast stones. [15] And he made in Jerusalem engines, invented by cunning men, to be on the towers and upon the bulwarks, to shoot arrows and great stones withal. And his name spread far abroad; for he was marvellously helped, till he was strong. [16] But when he was strong, his heart was lifted up to his destruction: for he transgressed against the LORD his God, and went into the temple of the LORD to burn incense upon the altar of incense. [17] And Azariah the priest went in after him, and with*

him fourscore priests of the L<small>ORD</small>, *that were valiant men: [18] And they withstood Uzziah the king, and said unto him, It appertaineth not unto thee, Uzziah, to burn incense unto the* L<small>ORD</small>, *but to the priests the sons of Aaron, that are consecrated to burn incense: go out of the sanctuary; for thou hast trespassed; neither shall it be for thine honour from the* L<small>ORD</small> *God. [19] Then Uzziah was wroth, and had a censer in his hand to burn incense: and while he was wroth with the priests, the leprosy even rose up in his forehead before the priests in the house of the* L<small>ORD</small>, *from beside the incense altar. [20] And Azariah the chief priest, and all the priests, looked upon him, and, behold, he was leprous in his forehead, and they thrust him out from thence; yea, himself hasted also to go out, because the* L<small>ORD</small> *had smitten him.*

2 CHRONICLES 26:14-20

INDEPENDENT OR GOD DEPENDENT?

In 2 Samuel 11, we see that David had become so prosperous, he decided to send other people to do what God had called him to do. It was obvious that he was bored, because he rose when the sun was going down. That means he wasn't doing anything.

And it came to pass, after the year was expired, at the time when kings go forth to battle, that David sent Joab, and his servants with him, and all Israel; and they destroyed the children of Ammon, and besieged Rabbah. But David tarried still at Jerusalem. [2] And it came to pass in an eveningtide, that David arose from off his bed, and walked upon the roof of the king's house: and from the roof he saw a woman washing herself; and the woman was very beautiful to look upon. [3] And David sent and enquired after the woman. And one said, Is not this Bathsheba, the daughter of Eliam, the wife of Uriah the Hittite? [4] And David sent messengers, and took her; and she came in unto him, and he lay with her.

2 SAMUEL 11:1-4

David started out God dependent but became independent of God because of prosperity. These scriptures made me aware that if the Lord multiplied my ministry and gave me more influence—reaching more and more people—it could lead to my destruction. I was fearful of that. Some of you may think that's strange, but I was afraid of success and what it could potentially do to me. Then one day, the Lord said to me, "I've been working on you for thirty-three years, and you just need to trust that I've prepared you for this." So, I had to overcome this fear and say, "Father, I'll take it and whatever comes with it."

Fear was holding me back. I hate to admit it, but part of it was just a sense of unworthiness. I knew that God loved me and carried my picture in His wallet, but I still had to deal with what other people thought of me. I just didn't feel worthy enough for God to use me. As I've said before, if I were God, I wouldn't have picked me.

GOD SEPARATED YOU

The Lord spoke to me in January 1973, just a few months after Jamie and I married. The Lord woke me up in the middle of the night and spoke to me from Jeremiah 1:4-8—

> *Then the word of the LORD came unto me, saying, [5] Before I formed thee in the belly I knew thee; and before thou camest forth out of the womb I sanctified thee, and I ordained thee a prophet unto the nations. [6] Then said I, Ah, Lord GOD! behold, I cannot speak: for I am a child. [7] But the LORD said unto me, Say not, I am a child: for thou shalt go to all that I shall send thee, and whatsoever I command thee thou shalt speak. [8] Be not afraid of their faces: for I am with thee to deliver thee, saith the LORD.*

Since that night, I've never told anyone that I couldn't speak. I didn't instantly get rid of my fear, but I started doing what God had spoken to me. Before He formed me in the womb, before I came forth out of my mother's belly, God had a purpose for me. Paul said the same thing in Galatians 1:15—*"But when it pleased God, who separated me from my mother's womb, and called me by his grace."*

We were created by God. Psalm 139:16 says that when we were still in our mothers' wombs, He knew all of our parts and they were written in His book. God knew everything about us. He created us and designed us for a specific purpose. It's not up to us to live our lives, discover that we have artistic talent or administrative talent or that we're people persons, and then look at our options and just pick and choose and do whatever we want to do.

God made you for a purpose, and it's up to you to find out what that purpose is. You cannot fulfill your purpose accidentally. It doesn't just happen by fate. You have to pursue the will of God in order to get it. It takes a revelation from God, because He will call you to do something beyond yourself; this way, you become God dependent. If you just look at your personality profile test to find out what you're suited for, you're going to miss God. There are things on the inside of you that He wants to accomplish.

God called me to do the exact thing I couldn't do—speak in front of millions of people. He called a hick from Texas to preach His Word. I've had people make fun of my voice to where some people have written in to our ministry, saying they thought I was Gomer Pyle! Another person once wrote to say that I was "as plain as dirt."

I understand exactly what they were talking about. I'm definitely not your typical minister. I am not a charismatic figure, yet God chose me. And, just by responding to Him, He has blessed me. He is using my life. People are alive today who would be dead if I wasn't doing what God told me to do. There are people who are beginning to understand the goodness of God, and their lives are being changed. There are miracles happening! You need to find your purpose. The only chance you have of reaching your full potential is to do what God created you to do.

HOLDING BACK THE BLESSINGS

In December 2001, the Lord dealt with me for about forty-five days until I figured out that I was limiting Him. Part of this process began as we looked for new office space because we had maxed out our 14,600-square-feet building. When we started looking for a new place, I was gone traveling and ministering while Jamie was with the realtor. When she picked me up from the airport, she showed me a couple of the places she had looked at and some of them were 30,000 square feet. Jamie said she thought that would probably hold our ministry forever. But as soon as she said that, I thought, *Oh, no, I forgot to tell Jamie that God had spoken to me and told me that one day we would have one of the largest ministries in the world.*

Jamie and I share everything; we talk about everything, but I realized that I hadn't yet told her about what the Lord had spoken to me. In the beginning of our ministry, I received so much criticism that I just quit talking about the things that God had put in my heart. Because I had been criticized so much in the past, I feared that Jamie, too, would reject my vision. When I realized I hadn't yet told her, I was shocked that I had let fear keep me from sharing this with her.

I had been on radio since 1976, but I had never allowed myself to think I was really influencing people, because I was afraid of being lifted up in pride. God showed me that I was limiting what He could do in my life because of my false humility—a sense of unworthiness—along with my fear of success.

One of the ways He showed me this was through a radio interview I did with Len and Cathy Mink. While I sat in an adjacent room, waiting on them to finish the news and weather report, they gave me an introduction that embarrassed me. They spoke about how the Lord used me, when they first got saved, to mold their lives and point them in the right direction. I had known of the Minks for years, but I had never thought that I could have been an influence in their lives. I shared this with them after the interview, and they were shocked. They reminded me that I had been teaching on over 100 radio stations for decades, so why wouldn't I believe that the Lord would have reached people through that?

Of course, what they said made sense, but I had never let myself think about how the Lord was using me, for fear of getting into pride. I was avoiding any temptation to become prideful by denying the obvious, which wasn't right either.

I had to confront these issues and deal with them. When I made that change in my heart and said "Praise God, I am going to do what God called me to do regardless of the potential for failure, rejection, persecution, or pride," within weeks, everything in our ministry changed. It began to explode!

The Lord showed me that He had been pouring all of these blessings out on me since He called me to minister forty-five years earlier, but I had built up a huge dam that was holding them back. When I finally yielded and said "All right, I'll do it" and started speaking faith over my ministry, it was like that dam burst and the power of God came gushing through!

Within weeks of taking the limits off God, I started to see miraculous results. This can also happen to you once you stop limiting what God wants to do in your life—whether it's because you have a fear of man or a fear of success or any other type of fear. God has a great plan for your life. He has an awesome purpose. Take the limits off God and watch His will come to pass in your life!

LESSON 5 • FEAR OF SUCCESS
OUTLINE

I.   Success has destroyed more people than hardship and failure ever has.
  A.   People often say things like, "When you're suffering and everything is wrong, it shows what's inside of you."

   Two things have I required of thee; deny me them not before I die: [8] Remove far from me vanity and lies: give me neither poverty nor riches; feed me with food convenient for me: [9] Lest I be full, and deny thee, and say, Who is the Lord? or lest I be poor, and steal, and take the name of my God in vain.

PROVERBS 30:7-9

  B.   A greater indication of what's on the inside of you is when everything is going well and you don't have to rely on God—how much do you study and pray then?
  C.   Moses told the Israelites to beware that when they came into all of their prosperity, they didn't forget that it was the Lord who gave them the power to get wealth so He could establish His covenant (Deut. 8:1-20).
  D.   Saul's life is a good example of this (1 Sam 15:17 and 26).
  E.   When Saul was little in his own eyes, God could use him, but when he became great in his own eyes, God couldn't use him.
  F.   Humility is necessary to walk with God, but Saul didn't continue to walk with God because he became proud and did his own thing.
  G.   God rejected him from being king because Saul limited what God wanted to do in his life.

   Pride goeth before destruction, and an haughty spirit before a fall.

PROVERBS 16:18

II.   In 2 Samuel 11, we see that David had become so prosperous, he decided to send other people to do what God had called him to do (2 Sam. 11:1-4).
  A.   David started out God dependent but became independent of God because of prosperity.
  B.   These scriptures made me aware that if the Lord multiplied my ministry and gave me more influence, it could lead to my destruction—I was afraid of success and what it could potentially do to me.
  C.   I had to overcome a fear of success and say, "Father, I'll take it and whatever comes with it."

III. Before He formed me in the womb, before I came forth out of my mother's belly, God had a purpose for me (Jer. 1:4-8).
   A. Paul said the same thing in Galatians 1:15: *"But when it pleased God, who separated me from my mother's womb, and called me by his grace."*
   B. God made you for a purpose, and it's up to you to find out what that purpose is.
   C. You have to pursue the will of God in order to get it.
   D. It takes a revelation from God, because He will call you to do something beyond yourself; this way, you become God dependent.
   E. There are things on the inside of you that He wants to accomplish.
   F. The only chance you have of reaching your full potential is to do what God created you to do.

IV. God showed me that I was limiting what He could do in my life because of my false humility—a sense of unworthiness—along with my fear of success.
   A. I had to confront these issues and deal with them.
   B. Within weeks of taking the limits off God, I started to see miraculous results.
   C. This can also happen to you once you stop limiting what God wants to do in your life— whether it's because you have a fear of man or a fear of success or any other type of fear.
   D. Take the limits off God and watch His will come to pass in your life!

LESSON 5 • FEAR OF SUCCESS
TEACHER'S GUIDE

1.　Success has destroyed more people than hardship and failure ever has. People often say things like, "When you're suffering and everything is wrong, it shows what's inside of you."

> *Two things have I required of thee; deny me them not before I die: [8] Remove far from me vanity and lies: give me neither poverty nor riches; feed me with food convenient for me: [9] Lest I be full, and deny thee, and say, Who is the LORD? or lest I be poor, and steal, and take the name of my God in vain.*
>
> PROVERBS 30:7-9

A greater indication of what's on the inside of us is when everything is going well and we don't have to rely on God—how much do we study and pray then? Moses told the Israelites to beware that when they came into all of their prosperity, they didn't forget that it was the Lord who gave them the power to get wealth so He could establish His covenant (Deut. 8:1-20). Saul's life is a good example of this (1 Sam. 15:17 and 26). When Saul was little in his own eyes, God could use him, but when he became great in his own eyes, God couldn't use him. Humility is necessary to walk with God, but Saul didn't continue to walk with God because he became proud and did his own thing. God rejected him from being king because Saul limited what God wanted to do in his life.

> *Pride goeth before destruction, and an haughty spirit before a fall.*
>
> PROVERBS 16:18

1a.　*Discussion question:* Why would success destroy more people than failure ever would?
　　Discussion question
1b.　*Discussion question:* Read Proverbs 30:7-9. What are some lessons you can learn from these verses?
　　Discussion question
1c.　When Saul was little in his own eyes, God could do what with him?
　　Use him
1d.　True or false: Humility is helpful, but not necessary to walk with God.
　　False

2.   In 2 Samuel 11, we see that David had become so prosperous, he decided to send other people to do what God had called him to do (2 Sam. 11:1-4). David started out God dependent but became independent of God because of prosperity. These scriptures made Andrew aware that if the Lord multiplied his ministry and gave him more influence, it could lead to his destruction—he was afraid of success and what it could potentially do to him. He had to overcome a fear of success and say, "Father, I'll take it and whatever comes with it."

2a.   David started out God dependent but became _____ because of _____.
   A.   Prosperous / God
   B.   Arrogant / pride
   C.   Independent / maturity
   D.   Humble / chastisement
   E.   Independent / prosperity
   E.   Independent / prosperity
2b.   Andrew feared that if Lord multiplied him and gave him more influence it could lead to what?
   His destruction
2c.   *Discussion question:* What are some ways to overcome a fear of success?
   Discussion question

3.   Before God formed Andrew in the womb, before he came forth out of his mother's belly, God had a purpose for him (Jer. 1:4-8). Paul said the same thing in Galatians 1:15: *"But when it pleased God, who separated me from my mother's womb, and called me by his grace."* God made us for a purpose, and it's up to us to find out what that purpose is. We have to pursue the will of God in order to get it. It takes a revelation from God, because He will call us to do something beyond ourselves; this way, we become God dependent. There are things on the inside of us that He wants to accomplish. The only chance we have of reaching our full potential is to do what God created us to do.

3a.   Fulfilling your purpose takes a _____ from God.
   Revelation
3b.   Why does God call you to do something beyond yourself that you can't do on your own?
   So you become God dependent
3c.   True or false: The only chance you have of reaching your full potential is to do what God created you to do.
   True

4.   God showed Andrew that he was limiting what God could do in his life because of Andrew's false humility—a sense of unworthiness—along with his fear of success. Andrew had to confront these issues and deal with them. Within weeks of taking the limits off God, he started to see miraculous results. This can also happen to us once we stop limiting what God wants to do in our lives—whether it's because we have a fear of man or a fear of success or any other type of fear. Let's take the limits off God and watch His will come to pass in our lives!

4a.   Which of the following things were limiting God in Andrew's life?
    A. A sense of unworthiness
    B. Fear of success
    C. False humility
    D. All of the above
    E. None of the above
    D. All of the above

4b.   *Discussion question:* What types of fears do you allow to hold you back and limit God?
    Discussion question

LESSON 5 • FEAR OF SUCCESS
DISCIPLESHIP QUESTIONS

1. *Discussion question:* Why would success destroy more people than failure ever would?
   _____
   _____
   _____

2. *Discussion question:* Read Proverbs 30:7-9. What are some lessons you can learn from these verses?
   _____
   _____
   _____

3. When Saul was little in his own eyes, God could do what with him?
   _____
   _____
   _____

4. True or false: Humility is helpful, but not necessary to walk with God.

5. David started out God dependent but became _____ because
   of _____.
   A. Prosperous / God
   B. Arrogant / pride
   C. Independent / maturity
   D. Humble / chastisement
   E. Independent / prosperity

6. Andrew feared that if Lord multiplied him and gave him more influence it could lead to what?
   _____
   _____
   _____

7. *Discussion question:* What are some ways to overcome a fear of success?

    _____

    _____

    _____

8. Fulfilling your purpose takes a _____ from God.

9. Why does God call you to do something beyond yourself that you can't do on your own?

    _____

    _____

    _____

10. True or false: The only chance you have of reaching your full potential is to do what God created you to do.

11. Which of the following things were limiting God in Andrew's life?
    A. A sense of unworthiness
    B. Fear of success
    C. False humility
    D. All of the above
    E. None of the above

12. *Discussion question:* What types of fears do you allow to hold you back and limit God?

    _____

    _____

    _____

LESSON 5 • FEAR OF SUCCESS

ANSWER KEY

1. *Discussion question*
2. *Discussion question*
3. Use him
4. False
5. E. Independent / prosperity
6. His destruction
7. *Discussion question*
8. Revelation
9. So you become God dependent
10. True
11. D. All of the above
12. *Discussion question*

LESSON 5 • FEAR OF SUCCESS
SCRIPTURES

PROVERBS 30:7-9

Two things have I required of thee; deny me them not before I die: [8] Remove far from me vanity and lies: give me neither poverty nor riches; feed me with food convenient for me: [9] Lest I be full, and deny thee, and say, Who is the LORD? or lest I be poor, and steal, and take the name of my God in vain.

DEUTERONOMY 8:1-20

All the commandments which I command thee this day shall ye observe to do, that ye may live, and multiply, and go in and possess the land which the LORD sware unto your fathers. [2] And thou shalt remember all the way which the LORD thy God led thee these forty years in the wilderness, to humble thee, and to prove thee, to know what was in thine heart, whether thou wouldest keep his commandments, or no. [3] And he humbled thee, and suffered thee to hunger, and fed thee with manna, which thou knewest not, neither did thy fathers know; that he might make thee know that man doth not live by bread only, but by every word that proceedeth out of the mouth of the LORD doth man live. [4] Thy raiment waxed not old upon thee, neither did thy foot swell, these forty years. [5] Thou shalt also consider in thine heart, that, as a man chasteneth his son, so the LORD thy God chasteneth thee. [6] Therefore thou shalt keep the commandments of the LORD thy God, to walk in his ways, and to fear him. [7] For the LORD thy God bringeth thee into a good land, a land of brooks of water, of fountains and depths that spring out of valleys and hills; [8] A land of wheat, and barley, and vines, and fig trees, and pomegranates; a land of oil olive, and honey; [9] A land wherein thou shalt eat bread without scarceness, thou shalt not lack any thing in it; a land whose stones are iron, and out of whose hills thou mayest dig brass. [10] When thou hast eaten and art full, then thou shalt bless the LORD thy God for the good land which he hath given thee. [11] Beware that thou forget not the LORD thy God, in not keeping his commandments, and his judgments, and his statutes, which I command thee this day: [12] Lest when thou hast eaten and art full, and hast built goodly houses, and dwelt therein; [13] And when thy herds and thy flocks multiply, and thy silver and thy gold is multiplied, and all that thou hast is multiplied; [14] Then thine heart be lifted up, and thou forget the LORD thy God, which brought thee forth out of the land of Egypt, from the house of bondage; [15] Who led thee through that great and terrible wilderness, wherein were fiery serpents, and scorpions, and drought, where there was no water; who brought thee forth water out of the rock of flint; [16] Who fed thee in the wilderness with manna, which thy fathers knew not, that he might humble thee, and that he might prove thee, to do thee good at thy latter end; [17] And thou say in thine heart, My power and the might of mine hand hath gotten me this wealth. [18] But thou shalt remember the LORD thy God: for it is he that giveth thee power to get wealth, that he may establish his covenant which he sware unto thy fathers, as it is this day. [19] And it shall be, if thou do at all forget the LORD thy God, and walk after other gods, and serve them, and worship them, I testify against you this day that ye shall surely perish. [20] As the nations which the LORD destroyeth before your face, so shall ye perish; because ye would not be obedient unto the voice of the LORD your God.

1 SAMUEL 15:17

And Samuel said, When thou wast little in thine own sight, wast thou not made the head of the tribes of Israel, and the LORD anointed thee king over Israel?

1 SAMUEL 15:26

And Samuel said unto Saul, I will not return with thee: for thou hast rejected the word of the LORD, and the LORD hath rejected thee from being king over Israel.

PROVERBS 16:18

Pride goeth before destruction, and an haughty spirit before a fall.

1 PETER 5:5

Likewise, ye younger, submit yourselves unto the elder. Yea, all of you be subject one to another, and be clothed with humility: for God resisteth the proud, and giveth grace to the humble.

2 CHRONICLES 26:14-20

And Uzziah prepared for them throughout all the host shields, and spears, and helmets, and habergeons, and bows, and slings to cast stones. [15] And he made in Jerusalem engines, invented by cunning men, to be on the towers and upon the bulwarks, to shoot arrows and great stones withal. And his name spread far abroad; for he was marvellously helped, till he was strong. [16] But when he was strong, his heart was lifted up to his destruction: for he transgressed against the LORD his God, and went into the temple of the LORD to burn incense upon the altar of incense. [17] And Azariah the priest went in after him, and with him fourscore priests of the LORD, that were valiant men: [18] And they withstood Uzziah the king, and said unto him, It appertaineth not unto thee, Uzziah, to burn incense unto the LORD, but to the priests the sons of Aaron, that are consecrated to burn incense: go out of the sanctuary; for thou hast trespassed; neither shall it be for thine honour from the LORD God. [19] Then Uzziah was wroth, and had a censer in his hand to burn incense: and while he was wroth with the priests, the leprosy even rose up in his forehead before the priests in the house of the LORD, from beside the incense altar. [20] And Azariah the chief priest, and all the priests, looked upon him, and, behold, he was leprous in his forehead, and they thrust him out from thence; yea, himself hasted also to go out, because the LORD had smitten him.

DON'T LIMIT GOD

2 SAMUEL 11:1-4

And it came to pass, after the year was expired, at the time when kings go forth to battle, that David sent Joab, and his servants with him, and all Israel; and they destroyed the children of Ammon, and besieged Rabbah. But David tarried still at Jerusalem. [2] And it came to pass in an eveningtide, that David arose from off his bed, and walked upon the roof of the king's house: and from the roof he saw a woman washing herself; and the woman was very beautiful to look upon. [3] And David sent and enquired after the woman. And one said, Is not this Bathsheba, the daughter of Eliam, the wife of Uriah the Hittite? [4] And David sent messengers, and took her; and she came in unto him, and he lay with her; for she was purified from her uncleanness: and she returned unto her house.

JEREMIAH 1:4-8

Then the word of the LORD came unto me, saying, [5] Before I formed thee in the belly I knew thee; and before thou camest forth out of the womb I sanctified thee, and I ordained thee a prophet unto the nations. [6] Then said I, Ah, LORD GOD! behold, I cannot speak: for I am a child. [7] But the LORD said unto me, Say not, I am a child: for thou shalt go to all that I shall send thee, and whatsoever I command thee thou shalt speak. [8] Be not afraid of their faces: for I am with thee to deliver thee, saith the LORD.

GALATIANS 1:15

But when it pleased God, who separated me from my mother's womb, and called me by his grace.

PSALM 139:16

Thine eyes did see my substance, yet being unperfect; and in thy book all my members were written, which in continuance were fashioned, when as yet there was none of them.

IMAGINATION

When I first called my staff together to tell them what the Lord had spoken to me, I told them I had an image on the inside of me of what I was *capable* of doing—and an image on the inside of me of what I was *incapable* of doing. We all have an image inside of us of what we can do (what we are capable of doing), along with what only God can do through us (what we are incapable of doing). This latter image serves as a ceiling, or limit, on what God can do in our lives.

We see ourselves a certain way, but we have to change that image if we don't want to limit God. I didn't know how long it would take to change the image of what I was incapable of doing—a week, a month, a year, or even longer—but I was determined to change it and start seeing myself doing what God told me to do!

God created you with an imagination, and you can't think without it. If I asked how many doors you have in your home, you probably wouldn't be able to answer that right away because you've never counted the number of doors in your house. You don't have this piece of information just filed away in your memory, yet you could count the number of doors in your home using your imagination. You could go through every room in your house and count the number of doors without seeing them with your physical eyes. You would engage your imagination to see them.

WE USE OUR IMAGINATIONS EVERY DAY

Most of us don't realize how much we use our imaginations, thinking they're just for kids. But we use our imaginations every moment of every day. We couldn't drive to work if we couldn't see how to get there in our minds. We also engage our imaginations when we "walk the aisles" to make a grocery list from home.

We often wrongly believe that using our imaginations is the same as fantasizing, but it isn't. *Imagination* is defined as "the act or power of forming a mental image of something not present to the senses or never before wholly perceived in reality" (*Merriam-Webster.com*). In other words, imagination is the ability to see something with our minds that we cannot see with our physical eyes.

Your imagination is essential. You cannot function without it! For example, you use your imagination when someone asks you for directions and you visualize the route in your mind. If someone asked you how to get to your house from the nearest freeway, you wouldn't have to drive there to give directions. You could picture the roads and guide that person by what you saw in your mind— your imagination. You could give landmarks along the way, along with approximate distances between streets. You are able to do this because you have internalized all of it in your imagination; you are looking at it through your imagination.

When it comes to God's direction for our lives, we have to use our imaginations to see those things come to pass. Many of us take great comfort in blaming others, our education, our skin color, or our status in life for the way things are; we might even blame our background or the fact we were abused as children. Even though we might have a million and one excuses, none of these external things control our lives. Our lives are the way they are today because of the way we have seen them or pictured them in our imaginations. The way we think determines the direction our lives will go.

WE THINK IN PICTURES

We don't remember most information given to us. That's why a lot of educational methods are not effective. Our imaginations, however, can help us understand abstract concepts like mathematics. For example, some people struggle with comprehending math, but a good teacher will illustrate math problems in a way that helps students understand. Instead of teaching "One plus one equals two, and two plus two equals four," it's better to teach " I've got two apples, and if I put two more with them, how many apples will I have?" By drawing a word picture, the teacher helps the students visualize the concept.

When you hear the word *apple*, you don't envision the letters "a-p-p-l-e." Instead, you see a mental image of an apple. Some of you might see a green apple while others may see a red one, but the word *apple* still brings an image of an apple to mind. I could change your picture of an apple by using specific words. For instance, if I said "A big, red, juicy apple," your mental image of the apple would change to envision these adjectives. Words paint pictures!

Nothing can be built without an imagination. Architects use blueprints to show builders how to construct what they have imagined. When we were designing buildings for our new campus in Woodland Park, Colorado, we spent hours discussing how we wanted the auditorium to look. Once we were able to picture what we wanted in our imaginations, the architects could draw up the blueprints for the builder.

In Vietnam, our water came from water blivetts. Most of you can't picture a water blivett, so you won't be able to remember it or describe it to others. Water blivetts are black cylinder-shaped rubber containers with brass ends that were flown in on helicopters in 250-, 500-, and 1,000-gallon sizes. Each of these containers had a spigot on the end that we used to fill our canteens. As the water came out, the atmospheric pressure would collapse the blivett, flattening it. Then the helicopter would pick it up and carry it away. This may not present a perfect picture of a water blivett, but at least now you have some idea of what one is because you have an image to attach it to—you have something you can "see."

Have you ever wondered why people get epiphanies when they go to Israel? It's not because it was where Jesus walked or because there's a special anointing there. That's not it at all! It's because, all of a sudden, they can see the things they tried to picture in their minds. Everything becomes more real. Being "on location" engages the imagination. Once people see it, the Word comes alive to them.

You have to get your imagination involved in order to take the limits off God. You can't see anything happen without your imagination. You have to use your imagination to start thinking and seeing bigger. If you can't see something on the inside, you won't be able to see it manifest in your life. If you can't see yourself healed or imagine yourself healthy, you won't see healing manifest in your body. Take the limits off God by using your imagination in a positive way to accomplish His purpose for your life!

WE USE OUR IMAGINATIONS TO REMEMBER THINGS

O Lord God of Abraham, Isaac, and of Israel, our fathers, keep this for ever in the imagination of the thoughts of the heart of thy people, and prepare their heart unto thee.

1 CHRONICLES 29:18

When David was close to dying, he called all of the people of Israel together and took up an offering to build the temple. David had given one or two billion dollars' worth of gold from his personal wealth toward the temple. When he did that, the rest of the nation rose up. The people were so touched by David's giving that they started giving—and all together, they took up an offering of over five billion dollars!

David began praising God and said, "God, who are we?" Then he went back and recounted how they had come out of Egypt as slaves but had gotten to where they were able to give such a generous offering. All they did was take the blessing that God had already given them and give it back. When David asked God to keep this forever in the imagination of the hearts of the people, he was saying, "Don't let them forget it!"

Memory is also tied to imagination—from simple things like remembering where we parked our cars, to recalling the neighborhoods we grew up in. Our memory functions off our imaginations. Most of us don't write down where we parked our cars every time we go somewhere; we just have a mental image of where we left it.

This is how we remember things. We can't remember anything we can't picture or imagine. We really can't understand something unless we can picture it in our minds. That's why people say a picture is worth a thousand words. If we can picture something, we can have it or do it!

CAN YOU SEE?

I once heard a story about a pastor's wife who was legally blind. Her glasses were so thick that they looked like the bottom of a soda bottle. A healing evangelist was preaching at their church one day, and she was trying to avoid him. Many people had prayed for her eyes in the past; however, she was never healed, so she didn't want to receive prayer again. But the healing evangelist cornered her at one of the services and said, "I want to pray for you."

He made her take her glasses off and commanded her eyes to be healed. When he was done, he asked, "Can you see?"

The woman started to open her eyes to check her vision, but the healing evangelist stopped her. "Shut your eyes!" he ordered. And she shut her eyes quickly.

"Can you see?" he asked. As soon as she started to open her eyes, he commanded, "Shut your eyes!"

When they repeated the same exchange a third time, she stood there, confused and with her eyes closed, wondering, *What is this man doing? How can I tell if I can see if I don't open my eyes?* Then she heard the evangelist say, "I didn't tell you to open your eyes; you have to see yourself seeing on the inside before you can see on the outside. You have to see yourself healed."

She stood there with her eyes closed, thinking about what he said. Within a few minutes, she understood. He was basically asking, "In your imagination, are you blind or can you see?"

She prayed in tongues for a while and finally said, "I can see myself seeing."

"Now open your eyes," he told her.

When she opened her eyes, her vision was perfect. She was healed!

HOW DO YOU SEE YOURSELF?

Today people talk about being over the hill at the age of forty. They look at sick people in their seventies or eighties and think they have to be like them one day. They start talking about and anticipating the problems they are going to have when they get older, and it becomes a self-fulfilling prophecy.

We need to see ourselves as God sees us. His vision for us is revealed in His Word. Earlier I talked about how Moses was 120 years old when he died, and his eyesight was not dim nor his natural force abated (Deut. 34:7). We have a superior covenant to the one Moses had, so if he could be healthy and live to be 120 years old, then we can too!

We have to change the way we think. We need to study the Word and imagine the truths God has given us until they paint a picture on the inside of us—until we see ourselves healthy, righteous, and full of peace and joy. We can never see anything happen on the outside unless we see it happen on the inside first!

Many of you are praying for big things to happen—restoration of your marriage, healing in your body, or prosperity in your finances. You are praying for these things, but you can't see them—and it's frustrating. But if you'll just meditate on the Word and allow it to paint a picture on the inside of you, it will come to pass. As a man thinks in his heart, so is he (Prov. 23:7).

Paul said, *"We walk by faith, not by sight"* (2 Cor. 5:7). As Christians, our imaginations should paint such a real picture that we live by what the Word says more than we live by what we can see with our physical eyes. We can do that. We have God Almighty living inside us!

Are you picturing what God's Word says about you? Can you see yourself healed? Can you see yourself prosperous? Can you see yourself doing the miracles Jesus did? If not, you need to meditate on the Word of God until you can see yourself doing these things. You need to change the way you see yourself. You need to see yourself as God sees you. You need to take the limits off and engage your imagination in order to see God's will for your life come to pass.

SEEING ON THE INSIDE

Jesus said, *"He that believeth on me, the works that I do shall he do also; and greater works than these shall he do; because I go unto my Father"* (John 14:12). I began the process of seeing things on the inside by meditating on every scripture where Jesus healed somebody or raised somebody from the dead. Then I closed my Bible, shut my eyes, and saw myself raising Lazarus from the dead. I saw myself raising

Jairus' daughter from the dead. Everything Jesus did, I saw myself do. I pictured what it would look like when Jesus said, *"Take ye away the stone"* (John 11:39). I was engaging my imagination.

I began believing it was possible to see people raised from the dead after reading what Jesus said in the Gospel of John. This inspired me to believe that God would do miracles through me. I thought about all of the miracles Jesus performed and said, "Father, can I raise someone from the dead?" I meditated on this so much that every night in my dreams, I raised a dozen people from the dead. I had dreams about going into morgues and emptying them out. After about six months, I actually saw a person raised from the dead with my physical eyes, but then ten or fifteen years went by before I saw this happen again. One day, I again felt inspired by God to start imagining people being raised from the dead, and pretty soon, I was dreaming about it again.

Then, one night, I got a phone call that my own son had died. He had been dead for four-and-a-half hours when I received the call. I just started thanking God for His goodness and magnifying Him above the circumstances. By the time I arrived at the hospital, my son had come back to life—but it wouldn't have happened if I hadn't been meditating on and imagining God's "raising-from-the-dead" power!

Before you see something happen on the outside, you have to see it on the inside. It has to become so real to you that you see yourself doing it. You won't see the miracle-power of God if you are defeated, discouraged, or depressed in your imagination. Stop limiting God with your imagination. Resurrect your imagination, and start using it in a positive way!

VAIN IMAGINATIONS

The imagination is a powerful force, but it has to be engaged. We have to be intentional about it. If we just put our imaginations on automatic, we will wind up being vain in our imaginations. Romans 1:21 says if we don't give honor and glory to God and aren't thankful, our imaginations will become vain and our foolish hearts will be darkened. We will be alienated from the life of God because of the blindness of our hearts.

A positive imagination is a byproduct of whether we have truly been thankful and have valued the things of God. Praising God and being thankful will cause our imaginations to come alive, and we will start seeing things differently than we have ever seen them. A vain imagination, however, conceives evil instead of being creative and conceiving good things.

Because that, when they knew God, they glorified him not as God, neither were thankful;
but became vain in their imaginations, and their foolish heart was darkened.

ROMANS 1:21

The word *"imagination"* is only used once in the Bible in a positive way: *"O Lord God of Abraham, Isaac, and of Israel, our fathers, keep this for ever in the imagination of the thoughts of the heart of thy people, and prepare their heart unto thee"* (1 Chr. 29:18). Every other time that imagination is mentioned, it is used in a negative way.

Did you know that God and His purposes on earth were challenged by the imagination of people? In Genesis 11:6, the Lord came down to see the Tower of Babel and basically said, "Come, let Us confuse the people's language because they are one, their speech is one, and now nothing they have imagined will be restrained from them." Nothing they had imagined would be restrained from them, so God confused their language to cause disunity and to stop them from progressing to a point where they could meet all of their own needs. God wanted them to be dependent on Him.

A foolish, darkened heart is a hardened heart, and once a person's heart is hardened, they become separated from the life of God (Eph. 4:18). It's tragic, but most people live somewhere between a vain, negative imagination and a hardened heart. They only imagine bad things, so when the doctor tells them they are going to die, they start planning their funerals. They see themselves dying and start to imagine what's going to happen when they are gone. Such a vain, negative imagination works against them and causes a hardened heart. Having a hard heart doesn't necessarily mean they aren't trying to love God or follow His will for their lives; it just means they don't understand how much God loves them apart from their behavior or performance.

People with hardened hearts only see and understand the Word of God with their brains. Moving beyond that stage takes time and effort. They have to start obeying God, meditating on His Word, glorifying Him, and being thankful. They must focus on God and what He has already done for them, instead of being focused on themselves. As they focus more on Him, instead of their imaginations being vain, they will come alive.

KEEP YOUR MIND STAYED ON HIM

We can't become who God says we are unless we can see ourselves as He sees us. We will become exactly what we imagine—whether that image is positive or negative. If we think we are failures, we will be. We have to deal with our imaginations and get them to line up with God's opinion of us.

We would be much better off if we spent time encouraging our imaginations. We can't let what other people say determine our identities or our futures. We need to find out what the Word says about us. Then we need to pray and let the Holy Spirit give us an image of what He wants us to do—and who He wants us to be.

> *Thou wilt keep him in perfect peace, whose mind is stayed on thee: because he trusteth in thee.*
>
> ISAIAH 26:3

Our imaginations have to be stayed upon the Lord. Many of us think, *Well, I am trying to keep my mind stayed on the Lord.* But are we keeping our *imaginations* stayed on the Lord? Are we picturing what God's Word says about us? When we don't realize how important it is to keep our imaginations stayed on the Lord, we will allow them to be turned against us, and we will only see negative things.

USE WHAT GOD HAS GIVEN YOU

Ephesians 4:17 says—

> *This I say therefore, and testify in the Lord, that ye henceforth walk not as other Gentiles walk, in the vanity of their mind.*

The word *"Gentiles"* in this verse is referring to nonbelievers—those who are not in covenant with God. Don't walk like a lost person in the vanity of your mind. Vanity of the mind means that you aren't using all that God has given you.

Science tells us that we use only 10 percent of our brains. I can guarantee that we are not using everything God has given us. As Christians, we need to start utilizing what God has given us. God gave us our imaginations. They are a powerful force! We shouldn't be like the lost who only use their imaginations to see negative things.

The world tends to gravitate toward the negative. Pessimists are people with a very vivid imagination, yet they imagine all the wrong things. They see a glass half full and call it half empty. They always see the negative side of things. They are still using their imaginations, but now their imaginations have become vain. Likewise, if we aren't thankful and glorifying God, our imaginations will also become vain. If we aren't glorifying God—putting worth and value on Him by praising and thanking Him for what we have—our imaginations will default to seeing the negative side of everything.

CHANGE THE IMAGE ON THE INSIDE OF YOU

A lot of people miss what God has for them. For example, even though some ask for healing, they still see themselves sick on the inside. They have been sick for so long that the sickness is not just in their bodies; it has also spread to their minds and their emotions. They even see themselves sick in their dreams. When they pray, they are hoping something will happen, but they don't really believe it on the inside. They don't see themselves healed. Their imaginations have become vain and are working against them, instead of for them. It's important that people have the right image on the inside.

Some children are told from a young age that they aren't wanted or that they will never amount to anything. Others are put down because of their skin color, lack of education, or socio-economic status. When people believe the negative words or ideas that are spoken over them, it forms an image on the inside of them of who they are and what they can do. That image serves as a ceiling that they can't rise above. Even though their talents and abilities could take them further, they don't allow them to. They somehow find a way to self-destruct!

I have a very good friend whose father was pretty hard on him as a kid. They had a lot of cars on their property, and his father would make him help work on the cars. His father would say, "You're so stupid. You can't screw a nut on a bolt without crossing the threads."

Over the years, as I have worked with my friend on a number of cars, it seems like every time he put a nut on a bolt, he would cross-thread it. He would put it on once and it would be okay, but then he would say, "I think I've cross-threaded it." So, he would take the nut off, put it back on, and repeat the process five or six times, trying to get it right. Eventually he would cross-thread the bolt, because he had a negative image painted on the inside of him that was still affecting him.

We have to change the image on the inside of us and start seeing ourselves through God's Word. Once I changed the image I had on the inside of me, I came to a place where I believed I could do anything I needed to do. Today I can see myself doing anything. I am like a cork. You could take me to the bottom of the ocean, and I would rise to the top, because I've renewed myself through my imagination. If we have vain imaginations and allow our imaginations to work against us instead of for us, then we will limit what God wants to do in our lives.

LESSON 6.1 • IMAGINATION
OUTLINE

I. We all have an image inside of us of what we can do (what we are capable of doing), along with what only God can do through us (what we are incapable of doing).
    A. This latter image serves as a ceiling, or limit, on what God can do in our lives.
    B. God created us with imaginations, and we can't think without them.
    C. Most of us don't realize how much we use our imaginations, thinking they're just for kids, but we use our imaginations every moment of every day.
    D. *Imagination* is defined as "the act or power of forming a mental image of something not present to the senses or never before wholly perceived in reality" (*Merriam-Webster.com*).
    E. In other words, imagination is the ability to see something with our minds that we cannot see with our physical eyes.
    F. When it comes to God's direction for our lives, we have to use our imaginations to see those things come to pass.
    G. Our lives are the way they are today because of the way we have seen them or pictured them in our imaginations—the way we think determines the direction our lives will go.

II. Words paint pictures!
    A. Nothing can be built without an imagination.
        i. Architects use blueprints to show builders how to construct what they have imagined.
    B. You can't see anything happen without your imagination.
    C. You have to use your imagination to start thinking and seeing bigger.
    D. If you can't see something on the inside, you won't be able to see it manifest in your life.

III. Memory is also tied to imagination.
    A. Our memory functions off our imaginations.
        i. Most of us don't write down where we parked our cars every time we go somewhere; we just have a mental image of where we left it.
    B. We can't remember anything we can't picture or imagine.
    C. We really can't understand something unless we can picture it in our minds.
    D. If we can picture something, we can have it or do it!

IV. God's vision for us is revealed in His Word.
   A. We have a superior covenant to the one Moses had, so if he could be healthy and live to be 120 years old (Deut. 34:7), then we can too!
   B. We have to change the way we think.
   C. We need to study the Word and imagine the truths God has given us until they paint a picture on the inside of us—until we see ourselves healthy, righteous, and full of peace and joy.
   D. As Christians, our imaginations should paint such a real picture that we live by what the Word says more than we live by what we can see with our physical eyes (2 Cor. 5:7).
   E. We can do that—we have God Almighty living inside us!

V. Before you see something happen on the outside, you have to see it on the inside.
   A. It has to become so real to you that you see yourself doing it.
   B. You won't see the miracle-power of God if you are defeated, discouraged, or depressed in your imagination.
   C. Resurrect your imagination, and start using it in a positive way!

VI. The imagination is a powerful force, but it has to be engaged.
   A. We have to be intentional about it—if we just put our imaginations on automatic, we will wind up being vain in our imaginations.
   B. A positive imagination is a byproduct of whether we have truly been thankful and have valued the things of God.
   C. A vain imagination, however, conceives evil instead of being creative and conceiving good things.

   Because that, when they knew God, they glorified him not as God, neither were thankful; but became vain in their imaginations, and their foolish heart was darkened.
   ROMANS 1:21

   D. A foolish, darkened heart is a hardened heart, and once a person's heart is hardened, they become separated from the life of God (Eph. 4:18).
   E. Having a hard heart doesn't necessarily mean they aren't trying to love God or follow His will for their lives; it just means they don't understand how much God loves them apart from their behavior or performance.
   F. People with hardened hearts must focus on God and what He has already done for them, instead of being focused on themselves.
   G. As they focus more on Him, instead of their imaginations being vain, they will come alive.

VII. We will become exactly what we imagine—whether that image is positive or negative.
   A. We would be much better off if we spent time encouraging our imaginations.
   B. We need to find out what the Word says about us and pray and let the Holy Spirit give us an image of what He wants us to do—and who He wants us to be.

> *Thou wilt keep him in perfect peace, whose mind is stayed on thee: because he trusteth in thee.*
>
> ISAIAH 26:3

   C. Many of us think, *Well, I am trying to keep my mind stayed on the Lord*, but are we keeping our *imaginations* stayed on the Lord?
   D. When we don't realize how important it is to keep our imaginations stayed on the Lord, we will allow them to be turned against us, and we will only see negative things.

VIII. Ephesians 4:17 says—

> *This I say therefore, and testify in the Lord, that ye henceforth walk not as other Gentiles walk, in the vanity of their mind.*

   A. Vanity of the mind means that we aren't using all that God has given us.
   B. God gave us our imaginations—they are a powerful force!
   C. We shouldn't be like the lost who only use their imaginations to see negative things.
   D. If we aren't glorifying God—putting worth and value on Him by praising and thanking Him for what we have—our imaginations will default to seeing the negative side of everything.

LESSON 6.1 • IMAGINATION
TEACHER'S GUIDE

1.   We all have an image inside of us of what we can do (what we are capable of doing), along with what only God can do through us (what we are incapable of doing). This latter image serves as a ceiling, or limit, on what God can do in our lives. God created us with imaginations, and we can't think without them. Most of us don't realize how much we use our imaginations, thinking they're just for kids, but we use our imaginations every moment of every day. *Imagination* is defined as "the act or power of forming a mental image of something not present to the senses or never before wholly perceived in reality" (*Merriam-Webster.com*). In other words, imagination is the ability to see something with our minds that we cannot see with our physical eyes. When it comes to God's direction for our lives, we have to use our imaginations to see those things come to pass. Our lives are the way they are today because of the way we have seen them or pictured them in our imaginations—the way we think determines the direction our lives will go.

1a.   What are the two images you have on the inside of you?
What you can do (what you are capable of doing) and what God can do through you (what you are incapable of doing)
1b.   What does the latter image serve as?
A ceiling, or limit, to what God can do in your life
1c.   *Discussion question:* Discuss the importance of imagination in relation to God's direction for your life.
Discussion question

2.   Words paint pictures! Nothing can be built without an imagination. Architects use blueprints to show builders how to construct what they have imagined. We can't see anything happen without our imaginations. We have to use our imaginations to start thinking and seeing bigger. If we can't see something on the inside, we won't be able to see it manifest in our lives.

2a.   _____ can be built without imagination.
Nothing
2b.   If you can't see something on the inside, you won't be able to what?
A.   See it manifest in your life
B.   Play Chinese checkers
C.   Do it on the inside
D.   All of the above
E.   None of the above
A.   See it manifest in your life

3.   Memory is also tied to imagination. Our memory functions off our imaginations. Most of us don't write down where we parked our cars every time we go somewhere; we just have a mental image of where we left it. We can't remember anything we can't picture or imagine. We really can't understand something unless we can picture it in our minds. If we can picture something, we can have it or do it!

3a.   True or false: Memory has nothing to do with imagination.
      False
3b.   If you can picture something, you can _____ it or _____ it!
      Have / do

4.   God's vision for us is revealed in His Word. We have a superior covenant to the one Moses had, so if he could be healthy and live to be 120 years old (Deut. 34:7), then we can too! We have to change the way we think. We need to study the Word and imagine the truths God has given us until they paint a picture on the inside of us—until we see ourselves healthy, righteous, and full of peace and joy. As Christians, our imaginations should paint such a real picture that we live by what the Word says more than we live by what we can see with our physical eyes (2 Cor. 5:7). We can do that—we have God Almighty living inside us!

4a.   *Discussion question:* What are some truths from God's Word that you are studying and allowing to paint a picture on the inside of you?
      Discussion question

5.   Before we see something happen on the outside, we have to see it on the inside. It has to become so real to us that we see ourselves doing it. We won't see the miracle-power of God if we are defeated, discouraged, or depressed in our imaginations. Let's resurrect our imaginations, and start using them in a positive way!

5a.   What you see on the inside of you has to become so real that what?
      You see yourself doing it
5b.   What must you do with your imagination?
      Resurrect it and start using it in a positive way

6.   The imagination is a powerful force, but it has to be engaged. We have to be intentional about it—if we just put our imaginations on automatic, we will wind up being vain in our imaginations. A positive imagination is a byproduct of whether we have truly been thankful and have valued the things of God. A vain imagination, however, conceives evil instead of being creative and conceiving good things.

> *Because that, when they knew God, they glorified him not as God, neither were thankful;*
> *but became vain in their imaginations, and their foolish heart was darkened.*
>
> ROMANS 1:21

A foolish, darkened heart is a hardened heart, and once a person's heart is hardened, they become separated from the life of God (Eph. 4:18). Having a hard heart doesn't necessarily mean they aren't trying to love God or follow His will for their lives; it just means they don't understand how much God loves them apart from their behavior or performance. People with hardened hearts must focus on God and what He has already done for them, instead of being focused on themselves. As they focus more on Him, instead of their imaginations being vain, they will come alive.

6a.   True or false: The imagination is a powerful force, but it has to be engaged.
       True
6b.   *Discussion question:* What lessons can you learn from Romans 1:21?
       Discussion question
6c.   What must people with hardened hearts focus on?
       A. Christian television
       B. God and what He has already done for them
       C. God and what they should be doing for Him
       D. All of the above
       E. None of the above
       B. God and what He has already done for them

7.   We will become exactly what we imagine—whether that image is positive or negative. We would be much better off if we spent time encouraging our imaginations. We need to find out what the Word says about us and pray and let the Holy Spirit give us an image of what He wants us to do—and who He wants us to be.

> *Thou wilt keep him in perfect peace, whose mind is stayed on thee: because he trusteth in thee.*
>
> ISAIAH 26:3

Many of us think, *Well, I am trying to keep my mind stayed on the Lord,* but are we keeping our *imaginations* stayed on the Lord? When we don't realize how important it is to keep our imaginations stayed on the Lord, we will allow them to be turned against us, and we will only see negative things.

7a.   You will become exactly what you imagine—whether that image is _____
        or _____.
        Positive / negative
7b.   *Discussion question:* Are you keeping your imagination stayed on the Lord?
        Discussion question
7c.   When you don't realize how important it is to keep your imagination stayed upon the Lord, what will happen?
        You will allow it to be turned against you, and you will only see negative things

8.   Ephesians 4:17 says—

> *This I say therefore, and testify in the Lord, that ye henceforth walk not as other Gentiles walk, in the vanity of their mind.*

Vanity of the mind means that we aren't using all that God has given us. God gave us our imaginations—they are a powerful force! We shouldn't be like the lost who only use their imaginations to see negative things. If we aren't glorifying God—putting worth and value on Him by praising and thanking Him for what we have—our imaginations will default to seeing the negative side of everything.

8a.   What does "vanity of the mind" mean?
        That you aren't using all that God has given you
8b.   *Discussion question:* Why shouldn't you and your imagination be like the lost?
        Discussion question

LESSON 6.1 • IMAGINATION
DISCIPLESHIP QUESTIONS

1. What are the two images you have on the inside of you?
    _____
    _____
    _____

2. What does the latter image serve as?
    _____
    _____
    _____

3. *Discussion question:* Discuss the importance of imagination in relation to God's direction for your life.
    _____
    _____
    _____

4. _____ can be built without imagination.

5. If you can't see something on the inside, you won't be able to what?
    A. See it manifest in your life
    B. Play Chinese checkers
    C. Do it on the inside
    D. All of the above
    E. None of the above

6. True or false: Memory has nothing to do with imagination.

7. If you can picture something, you can _____ it or _____ it!

8. *Discussion question:* What are some truths from God's Word that you are studying and allowing to paint a picture on the inside of you?

    _____

    _____

    _____

9. What you see on the inside of you has to become so real that what?

    _____

    _____

    _____

10. What must you do with your imagination?

    _____

    _____

    _____

11. True or false: The imagination is a powerful force, but it has to be engaged.

12. *Discussion question:* What lessons can you learn from Romans 1:21?

    _____

    _____

    _____

13. What must people with hardened hearts focus on?
    A. Christian television
    B. God and what He has already done for them
    C. God and what they should be doing for Him
    D. All of the above
    E. None of the above

14. You will become exactly what you imagine—whether that image is _____ or _____.

15. *Discussion question:* Are you keeping your imagination stayed on the Lord?

    _____

    _____

    _____

16. When you don't realize how important it is to keep your imagination stayed upon the Lord, what will happen?

_____

_____

_____

17. What does "vanity of the mind" mean?

_____

_____

_____

18. *Discussion question:* Why shouldn't you and your imagination be like the lost?

_____

_____

_____

LESSON 6.1 • IMAGINATION

ANSWER KEY

1. What you can do (what you are capable of doing) and what God can do through you (what you are incapable of doing)
2. A ceiling, or limit, to what God can do in your life
3. *Discussion question*
4. Nothing
5. A. See it manifest in your life
6. False
7. Have / do
8. *Discussion question*
9. You see yourself doing it
10. Resurrect it and start using it in a positive way
11. True
12. *Discussion question*
13. B. God and what He has already done for them
14. Positive / negative
15. *Discussion question*
16. You will allow it to be turned against you, and you will only see negative things
17. That you aren't using all that God has given you
18. *Discussion question*

LESSON 6.1 • IMAGINATION

SCRIPTURES

1 CHRONICLES 29:18

O LORD God of Abraham, Isaac, and of Israel, our fathers, keep this for ever in the imagination of the thoughts of the heart of thy people, and prepare their heart unto thee.

DEUTERONOMY 34:7

And Moses was an hundred and twenty years old when he died: his eye was not dim, nor his natural force abated.

PROVERBS 23:7

For as he thinketh in his heart, so is he: Eat and drink, saith he to thee; but his heart is not with thee.

2 CORINTHIANS 5:7

For we walk by faith, not by sight.

JOHN 14:12

Verily, verily, I say unto you, He that believeth on me, the works that I do shall he do also; and greater works than these shall he do; because I go unto my Father.

JOHN 11:39

Jesus said, Take ye away the stone. Martha, the sister of him that was dead, saith unto him, Lord, by this time he stinketh: for he hath been dead four days.

ROMANS 1:21

Because that, when they knew God, they glorified him not as God, neither were thankful; but became vain in their imaginations, and their foolish heart was darkened.

GENESIS 11:6

And the LORD said, Behold, the people is one, and they have all one language; and this they begin to do: and now nothing will be restrained from them, which they have imagined to do.

EPHESIANS 4:17-18

This I say therefore, and testify in the Lord, that ye henceforth walk not as other Gentiles walk, in the vanity of their mind, [18] Having the understanding darkened, being alienated from the life of God through the ignorance that is in them, because of the blindness of their heart.

ISAIAH 26:3

Thou wilt keep him in perfect peace, whose mind is stayed on thee: because he trusteth in thee.

IMAGINATION

The Hebrew word *yetser* (*yeser* in some concordances) was translated *"imagination"* four times in the Old Testament. *Yetser* means "conception" (*Strong's Concordance*). When a couple wants to have a baby, they can't just pray for one. A baby has to be conceived through a physical relationship. Babies don't come via a stork. A seed must be sown in the woman's womb.

The imagination is our spiritual womb. It's where we conceive God's miracle-working power. No imagination means no conception. If we can't conceive it—get it into our imaginations—it won't come to pass. In the spiritual realm, miracles don't come by being desperate or just having a need. If we conceive a miracle, we will give birth to it. Yet most of us are waiting for the stork to bring us our miracle. If we want to see something on the outside, it has to first be conceived in our imaginations. In other words, we have to see it on the inside before it gets birthed on the outside. That's how God flows through us.

We must glorify God and recognize what He has done in our lives. We need to be thankful and magnify God above our circumstances. We have to take control and begin to conceive the purposes of God in our imaginations. We need to let the plan that God has for us take root in our hearts, see ourselves fulfill it, and then watch as it comes to pass.

Our imaginations are powerful. If we understood this and began to consciously cooperate with how it works by spending time in the Word and letting it paint an image inside us, we would be able to see God's plans on the inside. We would become spiritually pregnant, and it would just be a matter of time until we gave it birth. It will happen!

YOUR IMAGINATION WILL WORK FOR YOU

We need to meditate on the Word of God and intentionally start training our imaginations. If we just sit around like couch potatoes, we will never become buff. Our muscles will never get stronger and bigger—they will atrophy. It's the same way with our imaginations. We need to use our imaginations in a positive way. We need to take a truth and meditate on it until we see it manifest in our lives.

I remember when I built a deck on my house. I would sit there for hours looking at nothing, trying to see what I wanted the deck to look like. Once I saw it, I could do it! I sat there with a pen and paper and counted how many braces and beams I needed. There wasn't anything physical to look at, but I was looking at it with my imagination.

How we see ourselves is important. We have to see ourselves as able to do or be whatever we are praying for. We won't see miracles come to pass if we don't believe that God can do miracles through us. It needs to become so real in our imaginations that we dream about it. A positive imagination will help erase all of the self-defeating ideas we have wrongly believed about ourselves. It will also help us imagine ourselves the way God sees us.

I CAN SEE MYSELF DOING ANYTHING

Today we send signals through the air for television broadcasts. Years ago, it was impossible to think that we could carry phones with us or have personal computers. My mother traveled in a covered wagon when she was three years old, yet she saw her first car, first telephone, and men walk on the moon! She saw all of this in one lifetime. Things are happening today that people have only dreamed of in years past. If we can imagine it, it can be done. There is a way to do it. It may take a lot of cumulative effort, but it can be done.

My brother was a mechanic. When he was fourteen years old, he could take a car apart down to the last bolt. He'd take it apart and put it back together just to see if he could do it. Because of that, he's always been a super mechanic. He was four-and-a-half years older than I was, so he tried to teach me a lot about cars. I didn't want to be just like my brother, though, so I rebelled and went the other way. As a result, I could barely screw a nut on a bolt.

When I got turned on to the Lord, I started saying that I can do all things. I started working on cars and fixing things while praying in tongues, not having a clue what I was doing. I just told myself that I knew I could do it. This changed the image I had on the inside of me, and today I'm at a place where I believe I can do anything I need to do. Now, whether I should do it is another thing. But I can see myself doing anything.

CONCEIVE THE WORD OF GOD

We have to meditate on the Word of God until we conceive something. We can't throw out a prayer like "O God, heal me" or "Supply this need" and never conceive what we are asking for from the Word. We have to develop a relationship with God by spending time studying and meditating on His Word.

If we have interaction with the Word of God, it will become alive and real to us. Then once we conceive it in our imaginations, we will receive it. Very few of us will do this because it would interfere with our television schedules. So, we just pray, beg, plead, and fast one week out of the month instead of living every day in the presence of God. That's not the way it works. We have to conceive what the Word says.

The building that our ministry currently occupies is 110,000 square feet, but when we bought the building, only 10,000 square feet were finished office space. The rest was an empty warehouse. After the architects drew up the plans and we were waiting for the funding to start on the construction, I had them place tape on the floor where all of the walls would be.

I spent hundreds of hours walking around those taped lines in that empty warehouse. I was using my imagination. I was *seeing* the walls in place and *picturing* how everything was going to look. I was *seeing* people inside the auditorium. In fact, I put a piece of plywood on top of several five-gallon buckets and stood on the platform and preached. No one was even in the building—it was nighttime, and the warehouse was dark—but I preached like the auditorium was filled to capacity.

I never stepped over the tape; I always entered where a door would be. Some people might think this is strange, but I was helping my imagination. I used my imagination to *see* what I was believing God for. On the day we held the dedication ceremony for our building, everyone was excited to see what God had done. A woman said to me, "You don't look very excited. Aren't you delighted to have the building completed?"

Of course, I was excited, but it was almost anticlimactic to see it with my eyes because I had already seen it in my heart. For more than a year, I had seen on the inside what just then became visible on the outside to the physical eye. By the time the construction was completed, I was ready to move on to the next task God had for me.

AIM FOR THE STARS

I've learned many things from Oral Roberts. Hearing him tell about the things God had spoken to him inspired my imagination. Within a matter of months after speaking with him, God led me into the next major step for our ministry. Being around people who talk about vision causes us to dream big also. Most of us think too small. We aim at nothing and hit it every time. We limit God in our lives. We need to aim for the stars, because even if we miss, we might hit the moon!

If we have needs, we should go to the Word and find the answer to our needs. Let's take those scriptures and meditate on them. The Bible says in 1 Peter 1:23 that we are *"born again, not of corruptible seed, but of incorruptible, by the word of God, which liveth and abideth for ever."* The Word is a seed. If we plant that seed in our spiritual wombs—our imaginations—we'll see it germinate. It will only be a matter of time until we see the birth!

UNDERSTANDING

Understanding is more than knowledge or the ability to recall a fact. A lot of us read the Bible with our heads instead of our imaginations or hearts. That's like chewing food but not swallowing it. The Word won't minister to us in its fullness unless we get it down to the level where we understand it. It isn't enough to merely hear the things of God; we have to meditate on the Word until it paints a picture—until we truly see what is happening.

> *The eyes of your understanding being enlightened; that ye may know what is the hope of his calling, and what the riches of the glory of his inheritance in the saints.*
>
> EPHESIANS 1:18

The word used here for *"understanding"* is the Greek work *dianoia*. This is a compound word that means "deep thought" (*Strong's Concordance*). It was also translated *"imagination"* in Luke 1:51. In other words, there's a difference between just thinking about things on the surface and having a deep thought, or understanding, about them.

We can get information, but information won't change our lives unless we understand it. That is what Matthew 13:19 says: *"When any one heareth the word of the kingdom, and understandeth it not, then cometh the wicked one, and catcheth away that which was sown in his heart. This is he which received seed by the way side."* Jesus said, "Those who receive seed (the Word) by the wayside are those who do not understand the Word, so Satan comes immediately to steal the Word from them." Understanding is the seed getting below the surface where it can germinate. It's deep thought. It's the imagination.

We cannot understand something if we can't picture it and see ourselves doing it. Many of us quote a scripture about God supplying all of their needs, like Philippians 4:19, but haven't meditated on it until we see ourselves as prosperous. Therefore, we keep ourselves from the very thing we're trying to receive.

Imagination is a very important concept to understand. It's one of the things that will allow us to fulfill God's will. We can't live at a surface-level understanding of the things of God. We have to go beyond the surface to the point where the Word of God literally changes the way we see things with our hearts.

HOPE

For we are saved by hope: but hope that is seen is not hope: for what a man seeth, why doth he yet hope for? [25] But if we hope for that we see not, then do we with patience wait for it.
ROMANS 8:24-25

Hope, according to Scripture, is seeing something that we can't physically see. We're not hoping for something if we can see it. Hope is our imagination working for us instead of against us. We need a strong sense of hope. *"Now faith is the substance of things hoped for, the evidence of things not seen"* (Heb. 11:1). Faith only provides what hope has already seen. Hope is the positive use of the imagination.

I heard Charles Capps tell a story about a thermostat one time. It was probably made up, but the story illustrates a good point. A man who was from the mountains had never been around modern conveniences. He went to a meeting in the city, and the meeting room became hot as it filled with hundreds of people. The man was fanning himself to cool down when he saw an usher turn a dial on a small box mounted on a wall. Shortly thereafter, he started to feel cool air blowing on him. He was overwhelmed, so he went and asked the usher what he did to make the air cold.

"What do you mean?" the usher asked.

"You turned that little thing on the wall, and cold air started blowing," the man said.

"Well, yeah, it's a thermostat."

"Can I get one of those?"

"Of course you can. They sell them at any hardware store."

The man was excited and went straight to the hardware store to buy a thermostat. When he got back to his cabin in the mountains, he mounted it on the wall, turned the dial, and sat down to wait for the cold air to come out. But, of course nothing happened because the thermostat had to be connected to an air conditioning system in order to work. A thermostat doesn't cool air on its own—it activates the power unit that cools the air.

Just like a thermostat can be turned to hot or cold, our imaginations can be negative, which is a pessimistic outlook on everything, or positive, which is what the Bible calls hope. Hope is to faith what a thermostat is to an air conditioning system. Hope turns on the ability of God, while faith is the power that makes things come to pass. Faith only produces what hope has already seen. If our imaginations are negative, we will see failure on the inside, leading us to experience failure on the outside. But if we are hoping and seeing a miracle in our hearts, we will turn on the power of God to see that miracle manifest in our lives.

Many of us try to use our power units, but we don't have any hope. Hope is what controls faith. For instance, in the area of healing, if we ever get a strong hope to where we take the Word and meditate on it until we see ourselves well, then every cell in our bodies will work to make us well. Once we see ourselves well, we will become well.

If we go to a doctor, one of the first things that doctor will do is tell us every negative thing they possibly can about our situations. They don't want to get our hopes up. But we *need* to get our hopes up! We ought to have our hopes going through the roof, because our faith can only produce what we hope for. A negative image will cause everything in us to work toward making that negative image a reality. We have to change the image inside us by creating hope. Hope comes through the Word of God (Rom. 15:4). This is the first step of faith.

God created you to be so much more than you are probably experiencing. You are likely going through this life half blind, only seeing with your natural eyes. If you try to run a race half blind, you are probably going to trip over something. Getting into the presence of God will allow you to see things in your imagination. Everything in the physical might be indicating one thing, but in your heart, the Word of God can paint a picture of something else. For instance, natural evidence might suggest that your business is going to fail, but you could have an image on the inside of you and know beyond a shadow of a doubt that it will succeed. Take the limits off. Conceive the miracle in your imagination—then watch it come to pass!

ANDREW'S RECOMMENDATIONS FOR FURTHER STUDY

Our *Healing Journeys, Volume 2* DVD tells the story of a woman named Merci Santos, who was healed of multiple sclerosis (MS). One of the things she said when she was in a wheelchair and everyone told her she would never walk again was that she just knew it wasn't true. She saw herself healed and knew that one day she would be. She needed someone to teach her about the Word and help her to activate her faith, but she saw herself well despite the fact that her symptoms were getting worse and worse. That is what hope is. Hope won't get you healed; it provides the motivation for your faith to get you healed. Today Merci is totally free of MS. She can run in the physical just as she saw herself doing in her imagination.

LESSON 6.2 • IMAGINATION
OUTLINE

IX. The Hebrew word *yetser* was translated *"imagination"* four times in the Old Testament.
   A. It means "conception" (*Strong's Concordance*).
   B. The imagination is our spiritual womb—it's where we conceive God's miracle-working power.
   C. No imagination means no conception.
   D. If we conceive a miracle, we will give birth to it.
   E. We have to take control and begin to conceive the purposes of God in our imagination.
   F. We would become spiritually pregnant, and it would just be a matter of time until we give birth—it will happen!

X. We need to meditate on the Word of God and intentionally start training our imaginations.
   A. How we see ourselves is important.
   B. We have to see ourselves as able to do or be whatever we are praying for.
   C. A positive imagination will help erase all of the self-defeating ideas we have wrongly believed about ourselves.

XI. We have to meditate on the Word of God until we conceive something.
   A. If we have interaction with the Word, it will become alive and real to us.
   B. Then once we conceive it in our imaginations, we will receive it.

XII. Being around people who talk about vision causes us to dream big also.
   A. Most of us think too small—we aim at nothing and hit it every time.
   B. If we have needs, we should go to the Word and find the answer to our needs.
   C. The Bible says in 1 Peter 1:23 that we are *"born again, not of corruptible seed, but of incorruptible, by the word of God, which liveth and abideth for ever."*
   D. The Word is a seed—if we plant that seed in our spiritual wombs (our imaginations), we'll see it germinate.

XIII. Understanding is more than knowledge or the ability to recall a fact.
   A. A lot of us read the Bible with our heads instead of our imaginations or hearts—that's like chewing food but not swallowing it.
   B. The Word won't minister to us in its fullness unless we get it down to the level where we understand it.

The eyes of your understanding being enlightened; that ye may know what is the hope of his calling, and what the riches of the glory of his inheritance in the saints.

EPHESIANS 1:18

C. The word used here for *"understanding"* is the Greek word *dianoia*, and this is a compound word that means "deep thought" (*Strong's Concordance*).

D. There's a difference between just thinking about things on the surface and having a deep thought, or understanding, about them.

E. That is what Matthew 13:19 says: *"When any one heareth the word of the kingdom, and understandeth it not, then cometh the wicked one, and catcheth away that which was sown in his heart. This is he which received seed by the way side."*

F. Understanding is the seed getting below the surface where it can germinate.

XIV. Hope, according to Scripture, is seeing something that we can't physically see.

For we are saved by hope: but hope that is seen is not hope: for what a man seeth, why doth he yet hope for? [25] But if we hope for that we see not, then do we with patience wait for it.

ROMANS 8:24-25

A. Hope is our imagination working for us instead of against us.

B. We need a strong sense of hope because faith only provides what hope has already seen (Heb. 11:1).

C. Just like a thermostat can be turned to hot or cold, our imaginations can be negative, which is a pessimistic outlook on everything, or positive, which is what the Bible calls hope.

D. Hope turns on the ability of God, while faith is the power that makes things come to pass.

E. If our imaginations are negative, we will see failure on the inside, leading us to experience failure on the outside.

F. If we are hoping and seeing a miracle in our hearts, it will turn on the power of God to see that miracle manifest in our lives.

G. Hope comes through the Word of God (Rom. 15:4), and this is the first step of faith.

XV. God created you to be so much more than you are probably experiencing.

A. You are likely going through this life half blind, only seeing with your natural eyes.

B. Everything in the physical might be indicating one thing, but in your heart, the Word of God can paint a picture of something else.

C. Take the limits off by conceiving the miracle in your imagination—then watch it come to pass!

ANDREW'S RECOMMENDATIONS FOR FURTHER STUDY

Our *Healing Journeys, Volume 2* DVD tells the story of a woman named Merci Santos, who was healed of multiple sclerosis (MS). One of the things she said when she was in a wheelchair and everyone told her she would never walk again was that she just knew it wasn't true. She saw herself healed and knew that one day she would be. She needed someone to teach her about the Word and help her to activate her faith, but she saw herself well despite the fact that her symptoms were getting worse and worse. That is what hope is. Hope won't get you healed; it provides the motivation for your faith to get you healed. Today Merci is totally free of MS. She can run in the physical just as she saw herself doing in her imagination.

LESSON 6.2 • IMAGINATION
TEACHER'S GUIDE

9.   The Hebrew word *yetser* was translated *"imagination"* four times in the Old Testament. It means "conception" (*Strong's Concordance*). The imagination is our spiritual womb—it's where we conceive God's miracle-working power. No imagination means no conception. If we conceive a miracle, we will give birth to it. We have to take control and begin to conceive the purposes of God in our imagination. We would become spiritually pregnant, and it would just be a matter of time until we give birth—it will happen!

9a.   The Hebrew word *yetser* means _____.
        Conception

9b.   No imagination means what?
        A. No job
        B. No problems
        C. No salvation experience
        D. No conception
        E. No worries
        D. No conception

9c.   *Discussion question:* What do you think it means to conceive the purposes of God in your imagination?
        Discussion question

10.   We need to meditate on the Word of God and intentionally start training our imaginations. How we see ourselves is important. We have to see ourselves as able to do or be whatever we are praying for. A positive imagination will help erase all of the self-defeating ideas we have wrongly believed about ourselves.

10a.   *Discussion question:* What steps do you feel you need to take to intentionally train your imagination?
        Discussion question

10b.   What will a positive imagination do for you?
        Help erase all of the self-defeating ideas you have wrongly believed about yourself

11.   We have to meditate on the Word of God until we conceive something. If we have interaction with the Word, it will become alive and real to us. Then once we conceive it in our imaginations, we will receive it.

11a. If you have interaction with the Word of God, it will become _____ and _____ to you.
       Alive / real

12.   Being around people who talk about vision causes us to dream big also. Most of us think too small—we aim at nothing and hit it every time. If we have needs, we should go to the Word and find the answer to our needs. The Bible says in 1 Peter 1:23 that we are *"born again, not of corruptible seed, but of incorruptible, by the word of God, which liveth and abideth for ever."* The Word is a seed—if we plant that seed in our spiritual wombs (our imaginations), we'll see it germinate.

12a. True or false: If you have a need, you should go to your family and find the answer to your need.
       False
12b. *Discussion question:* What is the difference between a corruptible seed and an incorruptible seed (i.e., the Word of God)?
       Discussion question

13.   Understanding is more than knowledge or the ability to recall a fact. A lot of us read the Bible with our heads instead of our imaginations or hearts—that's like chewing food but not swallowing it. The Word won't minister to us in its fullness unless we get it down to the level where we understand it.

> *The eyes of your understanding being enlightened; that ye may know what is the hope of his calling, and what the riches of the glory of his inheritance in the saints.*
>
> EPHESIANS 1:18

The word used here for *"understanding"* is the Greek word *dianoia*, and this is a compound word that means "deep thought" (*Strong's Concordance*). There's a difference between just thinking about things on the surface and having a deep thought, or understanding, about them. That is what Matthew 13:19 says: *"When any one heareth the word of the kingdom, and understandeth it not, then cometh the wicked one, and catcheth away that which was sown in his heart. This is he which received seed by the way side."* Understanding is the seed getting below the surface where it can germinate.

13a. The Word won't minister to you in its fullness unless you get it down where?
       To the level where you understand it
13b. *Discussion question:* What do you think is the difference between just thinking about things on the surface and having a deep thought, or understanding, about them?
       Discussion question

14. Hope, according to Scripture, is seeing something that we can't physically see.

> *For we are saved by hope: but hope that is seen is not hope: for what a man seeth, why doth he yet hope for? [25] But if we hope for that we see not, then do we with patience wait for it.*
> ROMANS 8:24-25

Hope is our imagination working for us instead of against us. We need a strong sense of hope because faith only provides what hope has already seen (Heb. 11:1). Just like a thermostat can be turned to hot or cold, our imaginations can be negative, which is a pessimistic outlook on everything, or positive, which is what the Bible calls hope. Hope turns on the ability of God, while faith is the power that makes things come to pass. If our imaginations are negative, we will see failure on the inside, leading us to experience failure on the outside. If we are hoping and seeing a miracle in our hearts, it will turn on the power of God to see that miracle manifest in our lives. Hope comes through the Word of God (Rom. 15:4), and this is the first step of faith.

14a. What is hope?
   A. What turns on the ability of God
   B. Your imagination working for you instead of against you
   C. Seeing something you can't physically see
   D. All of the above
   E. None of the above
   D. All of the above
14b. If your imagination is negative, what will happen?
   You will see failure on the inside, leading you to experience failure on the outside
14c. *Discussion question:* How have you witnessed the power of hope at work in your life?
   Discussion question
14d. Where does hope come from?
   Through the Word of God (Rom. 15:4)

15. God created us to be so much more than we are probably experiencing. We are likely going through this life half blind, only seeing with our natural eyes. Everything in the physical might be indicating one thing, but in our hearts, the Word of God can paint a picture of something else. Let's take the limits off by conceiving the miracle in our imaginations—then watch it come to pass!

15a. True or false: If you are only seeing with your natural eyes, you are half blind.
   True

LESSON 6.2 • IMAGINATION
DISCIPLESHIP QUESTIONS

19. The Hebrew word *yetser* means _____.

20. No imagination means what?
     A. No job
     B. No problems
     C. No salvation experience
     D. No conception
     E. No worries

21. *Discussion question:* What do you think it means to conceive the purposes of God in your imagination?

     _____
     _____
     _____

22. *Discussion question:* What steps do you feel you need to take to intentionally train your imagination?

     _____
     _____
     _____

23. What will a positive imagination do for you?

     _____
     _____
     _____

24. If you have interaction with the Word of God, it will become _____ and _____ to you.

25. True or false: If you have a need, you should go to your family and find the answer to your need.

26. *Discussion question:* What is the difference between a corruptible seed and an incorruptible seed (i.e., the Word of God)?

_____

_____

_____

27. The Word won't minister to you in its fullness unless you get it down where?

_____

_____

_____

28. *Discussion question:* What do you think is the difference between just thinking about things on the surface and having a deep thought, or understanding, about them?

_____

_____

_____

29. What is hope?
    A. What turns on the ability of God
    B. Your imagination working for you instead of against you
    C. Seeing something you can't physically see
    D. All of the above
    E. None of the above

30. If your imagination is negative, what will happen?

_____

_____

_____

31. *Discussion question:* How have you witnessed the power of hope at work in your life?

_____

_____

_____

32. Where does hope come from?

_____

_____

_____

33.   True or false: If you are only seeing with your natural eyes, you are half blind.

LESSON 6.2 • IMAGINATION
ANSWER KEY

19. Conception
20. D. No conception
21. *Discussion question*
22. *Discussion question*
23. Help erase all of the self-defeating ideas you have wrongly believed about yourself
24. Alive / real
25. False
26. *Discussion question*
27. To the level where you understand it
28. *Discussion question*
29. D. All of the above
30. You will see failure on the inside, leading you to experience failure on the outside
31. *Discussion question*
32. Through the Word of God (Rom. 15:4)
33. True

LESSON 6.2 • IMAGINATION
SCRIPTURES

1 PETER 1:23
Being born again, not of corruptible seed, but of incorruptible, by the word of God, which liveth and abideth for ever.

EPHESIANS 1:18
The eyes of your understanding being enlightened; that ye may know what is the hope of his calling, and what the riches of the glory of his inheritance in the saints.

LUKE 1:51
He hath shewed strength with his arm; he hath scattered the proud in the imagination of their hearts.

MATTHEW 13:19
When any one heareth the word of the kingdom, and understandeth it not, then cometh the wicked one, and catcheth away that which was sown in his heart. This is he which received seed by the way side.

PHILIPPIANS 4:19
But my God shall supply all your need according to his riches in glory by Christ Jesus.

ROMANS 8:24-25
For we are saved by hope: but hope that is seen is not hope: for what a man seeth, why doth he yet hope for? [25] But if we hope for that we see not, then do we with patience wait for it.

HEBREWS 11:1
Now faith is the substance of things hoped for, the evidence of things not seen.

ROMANS 15:4
For whatsoever things were written aforetime were written for our learning, that we through patience and comfort of the scriptures might have hope.

RECEIVE JESUS AS YOUR SAVIOR

Choosing to receive Jesus Christ as your Lord and Savior is the most important decision you'll ever make!

God's Word promises *"that if thou shalt confess with thy mouth the Lord Jesus, and shalt believe in thine heart that God hath raised him from the dead, thou shalt be saved. [10] For with the heart man believeth unto righteousness; and with the mouth confession is made unto salvation"* (Rom. 10:9-10). *"For whosoever shall call upon the name of the Lord shall be saved"* (Rom. 10:13).

By His grace, God has already done everything to provide salvation. Your part is simply to believe and receive.

Pray out loud, "Jesus, I confess that You are my Lord and Savior. I believe in my heart that God raised You from the dead. By faith in Your Word, I receive salvation now. Thank You for saving me!"

The very moment you commit your life to Jesus Christ, the truth of His Word instantly comes to pass in your spirit. Now that you're born again, there's a brand-new you!

It doesn't really matter whether you felt anything or not when you prayed to receive the Lord and His Spirit. If you believed in your heart that you received, then God's Word promises that you did. *"Therefore I say unto you, What things soever ye desire, when ye pray, believe that ye receive them, and ye shall have them"* (Mark 11:24). God always honors His Word. Believe it!

Please contact me and let me know that you've prayed to receive Jesus as your Savior or be filled with the Holy Spirit. I would like to rejoice with you and help you understand more fully what has taken place in your life. *Welcome to your new life!*

RECEIVE THE HOLY SPIRIT

As His child, your loving heavenly Father wants to give you the supernatural power you need to live this new life.

"For every one that asketh receiveth; and he that seeketh findeth; and to him that knocketh it shall be opened...how much more shall your heavenly Father give the Holy Spirit to them that ask him?" (Luke 11:10 and 13).

All you have to do is ask, believe, and receive!

Pray, "Father, I recognize my need for Your power to live this new life. Please fill me with Your Holy Spirit. By faith, I receive it right now! Thank You for baptizing me! Holy Spirit, You are welcome in my life!"

Congratulations—now you're filled with God's supernatural power!

Some syllables from a language you don't recognize will rise up from your heart to your mouth (1 Cor. 14:14). As you speak them out loud by faith, you're releasing God's power from within and building yourself up in the spirit (1 Cor. 14:4). You can do this whenever and wherever you like!

It doesn't really matter whether you felt anything or not when you prayed to receive the Lord and His Spirit. If you believed in your heart that you received, then God's Word promises that you did. *"Therefore I say unto you, What things soever ye desire, when ye pray, believe that ye receive them, and ye shall have them"* (Mark 11:24). God always honors His Word. Believe it!

Please contact me and let me know that you've prayed to receive Jesus as your Savior or be filled with the Holy Spirit. I would like to rejoice with you and help you understand more fully what has taken place in your life. *Welcome to your new life!*

ANDREW'S TEACHING RECOMMENDATIONS IN THIS STUDY GUIDE

LESSON 3.1

How to Find, Follow, and Fulfill God's Will

Most people have lost a sense of destiny, God's will for their lives. This revelatory teaching will help change that.

How to Find God's Will
Item Code: 1066-C 5-CD series / Item Code: 1066-D DVD series

How to Follow God's Will
Item Code: 1067-C 5-CD series / Item Code: 1067-D DVD series

How to Fulfill God's Will
Item Code: 1068-C 5-CD series / Item Code: 1068-D DVD series

How to Find, Follow, and Fulfill God's Will
Item Code: 335 Paperback book / Item Code: 756 Spanish book

How to Find God's Will
Item Code: 435 Study guide

How to Follow God's Will
Item Code: 436 Study guide

How to Fulfill God's Will
Item Code: 437 Study guide

LESSON 3.2

Effortless Change

Everyone has areas in their lives they want to change. Trying to change from the outside in is difficult. Inside out is effortless. Learn why.

Item Code: 1018-C 4-CD series / Item Code: 1018-D DVD series
Item Code: 331 Paperback book / Item Code: 742 Spanish book
Item Code: 431 Study guide

LESSON 6.2

Healing Journeys, Volume 2

Recorded here are five stories of the power of God's Word working in the lives of ordinary people. They all came to understand what God has already done for them through Jesus. Their stories will touch your heart and build your faith.

Item Code: 3008-D DVD